W9-BXV-472

"Most experts agree that anxiety and the closely related emotion of fear are fundamental to the human condition, and serve a valuable function by helping us avoid danger, adapt, and even plan for the future. And yet in our society individuals spend billions of dollars yearly to rid themselves of anxiety. The problem is that these fundamental emotions so necessary for our survival become excessive and pervasive in some individuals to the extent that their lives become paralyzed. Fortunately, our understanding of the nature of these emotions has advanced dramatically in the past several decades. Now, two outstanding young clinicians and scientists studying the nature and treatment of anxiety have distilled their cutting-edge knowledge to provide an integrative, easy-to-read and apply program for excessive anxiety and fear. Representing the latest and most effective techniques available, every individual suffering from anxiety will benefit by becoming acquainted with this program."

> —**David H. Barlow PhD, ABPP**, professor of psychology and psychiatry Emeritus at Boston University, and founder and director Emeritus of the Center for Anxiety and Related Disorders

"In mental health treatment, there is an increasing appreciation of the importance of emotion regulation—the skills that allow people to effectively cope with painful feelings—and the fact that people can learn more effective strategies for emotion regulation. In *Don't Let Your Anxiety Run Your Life*, David Klemanski and Joshua Curtiss take the reader step by step through the emerging science of emotion regulation, and illustrate how to apply that knowledge to everyday life. I heartily recommend this book for anyone who wants to master unwanted anxiety, and I anticipate that a lot of readers are going to find it extremely helpful."

> —**David F. Tolin, PhD, ABPP**, author of *Face Your Fears*

don't let your anxiety run your life

USING THE SCIENCE OF EMOTION REGULATION & MINDFULNESS TO OVERCOME FEAR & WORRY

DAVID H. KLEMANSKI, PsyD
JOSHUA E. CURTISS, MA

New Harbinger Publications, Inc.

Publisher's Note

This publication is designed to provide accurate and authoritative information in regard to the subject matter covered. It is sold with the understanding that the publisher is not engaged in rendering psychological, financial, legal, or other professional services. If expert assistance or counseling is needed, the services of a competent professional should be sought.

Distributed in Canada by Raincoast Books

Copyright © 2016 by David H. Klemanski and Joshua E. Curtiss
New Harbinger Publications, Inc.
5674 Shattuck Avenue
Oakland, CA 94609
www.newharbinger.com

Cover design by Sara Christian; Interior design by Michele Waters-Kermes; Acquired by Melissa Valentine; Edited by Will DeRooy

All Rights Reserved

Library of Congress Cataloging-in-Publication Data

Names: Klemanski, David H., author. | Curtiss, Joshua E., author.
Title: Don't let your anxiety run your life : using the science of emotion regulation and mindfulness to overcome fear and worry / David H. Klemanski, Joshua E Curtiss ; foreword by Stefan G Hofmann.
Description: Oakland, CA : New Harbinger Publications, 2016. | Includes bibliographical references.
Identifiers: LCCN 2016001939 (print) | LCCN 2016004497 (ebook) | ISBN 9781626254169 (paperback) | ISBN 9781626254176 (pdf e-book) | ISBN 9781626254183 (epub) | ISBN 9781626254176 (PDF e-book) | ISBN 9781626254183 (ePub)
Subjects: LCSH: Anxiety. | Mindfulness (Psychology) | Mind and body. | BISAC: SELF-HELP / Anxieties & Phobias. | PSYCHOLOGY / Emotions. | BODY, MIND & SPIRIT / Meditation.
Classification: LCC BF575.A6 .K584 2016 (print) | LCC BF575.A6 (ebook) | DDC 152.4/6--dc23
LC record available at http://lccn.loc.gov/2016001939

18   17   16

10   9   8   7   6   5   4   3   2   1   First Printing

Contents

Foreword   v

Introduction: Understanding Your Anxiety   1

1   Linking Anxiety, Emotion, and Mindfulness   17

2   Overcoming Attention Biases   43

3   Confronting Your Anxiety   69

4   Thinking Traps   97

5   Emotional Inflexibility   115

6   Information Overload   137

7   Feeling Bad Is Actually Good   153

8   Unhelpful Habits   171

9   Emotional Avoidance   181

10   Making a Habit of Mindfulness and
Emotion Regulation   197

Acknowledgments   207

References   209

Foreword

Fear and anxiety are fundamental aspects of human existence. Virtually every student of the human condition, from the ancient Greek philosophers to Sigmund Freud to contemporary theorists of psychology, has tried to make sense of these experiences. Unlike other species, humans spend a lot of time thinking about past failures and worrying about possible future events. If we feel our future is uncertain, we experience anxiety.

Anxiety is a future-oriented mood state associated with, or even caused by, worrisome thought processes. When we are anxious, our mind is focused on the future and on the things that could go wrong. To some extent this can be adaptive, because it helps us prepare for the future and avoid undesirable situations: it motivates us to buy insurance, plan for our retirement, and save money for our children's college education. But this same ability to anticipate future events comes at an emotional cost.

The same is true when we start ruminating about past events. Learning from our past failures is adaptive, but ruminating about the past is not.

Worrying about the future and ruminating about the past take us away from the present moment. Rumination and worrying are characteristic features of debilitating anxiety and depression. Anxiety disorders are some of the most common psychiatric conditions, next to mood disorders and substance use problems.

Although treatments for anxiety disorders are reasonably effective, there's clearly still room for improvement. Modern emotion research provides some concrete and novel methods of enhancing treatment for anxiety and related problems. In this elegant book, a highly accessible and informative text for anybody who struggles with anxiety, David Klemanski and Joshua Curtiss discuss some of these concrete guidelines and encourage you to effectively deal with fear and anxiety while experiencing life as it happens. The authors clearly articulate specific strategies for overcoming fear and anxiety, based on modern emotion research. These strategies include identifying and targeting maladaptive thought processes, enhancing adaptive emotion regulation strategies, and changing maladaptive habits. Mindfulness-based practices take center stage. Mindfulness is difficult to define and measure but relatively easy to practice. These strategies encourage you to pay attention to the present moment without judging it. As a result, you will learn how to live life in the present moment and let go of maladaptive thoughts that are linked to fear and anxiety.

This superb text will guide you through some basic and effective steps: pay attention to your anxiety, confront it, avoid thinking traps, flexibly respond to your emotions, accept your emotions, develop adaptive habits, and abandon maladaptive habits. Embracing these strategies will give you, the reader, the opportunity to distance yourself from your anxiety and your immediate impulse to act on your feelings. Applying these strategies will teach you how to be reflective, rather than reactive, toward your anxiety. You will learn how to exert control over your anxiety rather than being controlled by it. As a result, you may find a way to live your life in the here and now, rather than making other plans.

Time is precious. You have only one life to live and you can choose how you spend your time on this earth. You may choose to continue your maladaptive habits, resulting in anxiety and depression, or you may choose to take charge of your life and begin to control your anxiety. The choice is yours. If you choose the latter, continue reading this book and implement the strategies that are discussed. You have nothing to lose but your anxiety.

—Stefan G. Hofmann, PhD
   Professor of Psychology
   Department of Psychological and Brain Sciences
   Boston University
   www.bostonanxiety.org
   Author, *Emotion in Therapy: From Science to Practice*
   (Guilford Press, 2016)

introduction

Understanding Your Anxiety

Anxiety is an undeniable part of human life. Every living person on this planet, at some point in his or her life, has experienced anxiety. In fact, many people feel anxious on a daily basis, including members of your family, your friends, and your colleagues at work or school. Some people panic at the sight of an insect or rodent; others anxiously dread giving a speech or talking on the telephone. Some people chronically worry about "worst-case scenarios," while others fear leaving the relative safety of their home or encountering reminders of traumatic events that occurred in their past. Almost everything in life has the potential to make you feel anxious, but *only if you let it!* In other words, it's entirely possible to skillfully manage your anxiety by examining the relationships you have to your fears and worries *and* embracing them (rather than avoiding them!). Admittedly, this isn't easy, and we can't guarantee that you will never feel excessively anxious again, but we do pledge to help you master your anxiety so that you will feel more capable and in control of your daily life.

This book is intended to teach you about the science of mindfully managing your emotions in order to reduce your anxiety. In turn, this will help you change your relationship to your fears and worries and ultimately help you confront your anxiety. To accomplish this, we will provide you with several science-based strategies that emphasize the use of both mindfulness and emotion regulation, with the ultimate goal of helping you develop a more balanced and fulfilling life.

Overview of the Book

This book is based on two major psychotherapy techniques—mindfulness and emotion regulation—for reducing your own symptoms of anxiety by mindfully regulating your emotions. We will provide you with an integrated model of mindfulness and emotion regulation for reducing and managing your anxiety symptoms. To accomplish this, we will rely on modern psychological science to inform you about specific strategies that you can use to reduce your symptoms of anxiety, increase your daily functioning, and improve your quality of life. Although we recognize that the science of emotions is constantly evolving, we will provide you with skills and strategies based in well-grounded and enduring research so that you can mindfully regulate your emotions.

First, we will focus on the nature of anxiety and on the integration of theory and application of mindfulness and emotion regulation techniques. Then, we will review specific scientific principles and cutting-edge research on evidence-based interventions and provide the rationale for using self-directed techniques to outsmart your anxiety. By reading this book, you will learn how to *mindfully*:

- Pay attention to your anxiety

- Confront, rather than avoid, your anxiety

- Avoid common thinking traps

- Respond to your emotions in a flexible way

- Reduce conscious and unconscious threats to your emotional well-being

- Accept your emotions

- Develop adaptive habits for long-term regulation of your emotions

- Let go of safety behaviors and avoidance strategies

- Learn the integrated model of emotion regulation and mindfulness to successfully overcome your anxiety

This introduction will familiarize you with key concepts, including definitions, basic information, and examples of anxiety, emotion regulation, and mindfulness.

What Is Anxiety?

Anxiety is a negative mood state often accompanied by physical symptoms referred to as *physiological arousal*. This negative mood state is further characterized by nervousness, apprehension, and negative beliefs about the future, as well as emotional responses (such as fear, sadness, and anger) and behavioral responses (such as avoiding situations or objects that make you anxious). For example, if, while you were relaxing in a chair, a wasp landed on your arm, you might have anxious thoughts, such as *I don't want to get stung!* You might feel extremely fearful and experience a number of physical symptoms, such as increased heart rate or heart palpitations, shortness of breath, and muscle tension. You might even behave erratically—you might leap from your chair to run for safety, you might scream, or you might flail your arms to encourage the wasp to fly away.

Using a different example, imagine that you are driving on the highway and police lights suddenly show up in your rearview mirror. What specifically would you think? How would you behave? And how would your body react? Take a few moments to think about each of these questions or record your responses on a piece of paper. Your response to this anxiety-provoking scenario would entirely depend on *how you thought* about the situation and *how you reacted* to it.

Anxiety is a highly subjective experience, meaning it's different for each person. In addition, anxiety can range in intensity, meaning some people experience little to no anxiety in certain situations, whereas others experience excessive anxiety. When anxiety becomes excessive or out of control, it can quickly become problematic and affect your ability to function. If you have ever experienced problematic anxiety, you are certainly not alone! Almost everyone has at one point or another. However, if your anxiety has been present for a long time, if it causes you distress or if you avoid anxiety-provoking objects or situations altogether, and if it considerably interferes with your functioning, your anxiety may be the symptom of a psychological disorder. There are three broad categories of diagnosable anxiety conditions, all of which are treatable:

- Anxiety disorders (specific phobias, social anxiety disorder, panic disorder, agoraphobia, and generalized anxiety disorder)

- Obsessive-compulsive and related disorders

- Trauma- and stressor-related disorders

A word of caution: Although these disorders may sound straightforward, we encourage you *not* to diagnose yourself. Instead, seek advice from a mental health professional about how to best diagnose and address your anxiety.

What Is Emotion Regulation?

Have you ever been so anxious that you started shaking or trembling? Have you ever hyperventilated or burst into tears when you didn't feel up to performing a specific task? Have you ever angrily ranted about something that made you anxious? These types of experiences are usually a sign that your emotions are—at least temporarily—not well regulated. In psychology, *emotion regulation* describes the mental and behavioral processes by which people influence their own and others' feelings. Essentially, emotion regulation refers to how you try to influence what you feel, when you feel it, and how you experience and express it (Gross 2008).

Current scientific theories on emotions and how people regulate them emphasize that emotions can be both helpful and hurtful. On one hand, your emotions can facilitate your relationships and interpersonal interactions, heighten your memory of important events, or even help you behave in a certain way; on the other hand, your emotions can occur at the wrong time of day, come on too strongly, or be inappropriate to a situation. Depending on the context, especially in situations in which you feel anxious or fearful, it may be advantageous to change what, when, and how you are feeling by purposefully trying to influence your emotional response.

What Is Mindfulness?

Have you ever driven to the store and, once you got there, realized that you could remember very little about your trip? Or have you ever read a book or watched a television program only to notice that you couldn't remember specific details? Or perhaps you were trying to focus on a work or school project, but you felt distracted by your worries about an upcoming experience, such as a dentist appointment! These are common examples of operating on autopilot, or, more technically, acting without full present-moment awareness. The opposite of autopilot is mindfulness. *Mindfulness* is defined as "paying attention…on purpose, in the present moment, and nonjudgmentally" (Kabat-Zinn 1994, 4). In essence, mindfulness enables you to pay greater attention to both your inner self—your thoughts, feelings, and bodily sensations—and your current environment. Mindfulness is *not* a way to make yourself feel better, per se, but by cultivating a mindful approach to your anxiety, you will be better able to confront and manage your thoughts, emotions, and physiological symptoms in anxiety-provoking situations.

Hailing from ancient traditions, "mindfulness" refers to a transformative shift in perspective that facilitates a distanced, nonjudgmental relationship to your emotions. Practitioners of mindfulness sometimes call this "bare attention." It entails fostering enhanced awareness of your emotions and the surrounding environment, along with a nonjudgmental acceptance of that experience. Rather than consciously attempting to change the nature of your thoughts or experiences, mindfulness helps you embrace your experience with equanimity and allow thoughts and feelings to pass through your mind without reacting to them.

Contemporary research supports the potential therapeutic value of mindfulness-based techniques for many kinds of psychological difficulties and disorders. In fact, mindfulness has become the basis for some psychological treatments, such as mindfulness-based stress reduction. There's increasing evidence to support the effectiveness of mindfulness-based therapies (Hofmann et al. 2010) and the presence of mindfulness deficits in anxiety disorders (Curtiss and Klemanski 2014b).

Mindfulness has been consistently associated with lower rates of anxiety and a greater sense of well-being. Treatments for anxiety that incorporate aspects of mindfulness practice have been very successful in helping people combat anxiety. Mindfulness-based therapies foster a certain mind-set that promotes the use of skills for overcoming distressing thinking styles, increasing personally meaningful behaviors, and flexibly handling emotions. Widespread acceptance of mindfulness principles within the mental health care profession has allowed researchers to figure out that mindfulness leads to a decrease in anxiety and an increase in overall quality of life partly because of its ability to promote helpful emotion regulation.

Over time, and as you incorporate mindfulness into your life, it will very likely bring about long-term changes in your mood, your sense of well-being, and your quality of life. It can result in lower levels of unpleasant feelings and higher levels of positive feelings, both in intensity and in frequency (Brown and Ryan 2003; Ortner, Kilner, and Zelazo 2007; Chambers, Lo, and Allen 2008), and it can reduce mental and physical stress (Hoffman et al. 2010). Mindfulness is also associated with enhanced immune functioning, as well as increased satisfaction in relationships (Barnes et al. 2007; Wachs and Cordova 2007).

A question that commonly comes up about mindfulness is related to its origin and its use in treating anxiety and other psychological conditions. Although mindfulness is rooted in Eastern meditative traditions, it neither represents a foreign cultural ideology nor emphasizes a religious philosophy. We will discuss mindfulness according to current scientific theories and their applicability to managing emotions and anxiety. This book will also provide you with guided mindfulness practices that have direct therapeutic value and that complement the skills reviewed in each chapter. In chapter 1, we will review mindfulness in greater depth, but if you still have questions, we encourage you to research on your own the value of adopting a mindful approach to managing anxiety and anxiety-related disorders.

How Emotion Regulation and Mindfulness Can Help You Outsmart Your Anxiety

A striking fact about these two fields of psychological research (emotion regulation and mindfulness) is that they share a number of things in common. Taken together, they can provide a very powerful framework for helping people gain mastery over the dysfunctional management of emotions. Both emotion regulation and mindfulness promote awareness and acceptance of emotions, but they do so in different, yet complementary, ways.

Research on emotion regulation suggests that the use of certain strategies in appropriate contexts can facilitate the healthy expression and experience of emotions. Not all strategies are equally helpful, however; some responses to emotions can have negative long-term consequences, despite their seeming benefit. Take worry, for instance. Initially, it might seem like a good idea to worry about some potential mishap or something that can go wrong in your life. Spending a great deal of effort to scrutinize how an event might play out can make you believe that you will be well prepared to better handle the source of your concerns. Even though this type of technique is a direct way of responding to discomfort and seems proactive, which is often the chief goal of successful emotion regulation, it can be insidiously harmful. Worry reflects a *repetitive thinking style* that promotes both overly judgmental reactions to your concerns and unwanted emotions. This is completely opposed to the central tenets of mindfulness.

Integrating emotion regulation and mindfulness establishes a comprehensive framework that tells us *what* strategies work (emotion regulation) and *when* and *how* to employ them (mindfulness). Take the strategy of "expressive suppression," for example, or concealing outward expression of your emotions. In the long term, this overly reactive strategy, which entails conscious efforts to banish an emotional experience from your mind because you judge it to be bad, is generally dysfunctional. It violates many core principles of helpful emotion regulation and mindfulness, and over time it can lead to sustained levels of distress. But there are ways in which expressive suppression can be modified within a healthier framework. Let's consider them.

Imagine that you are experiencing anger in a public place. The overall goal remains the same as with expressive suppression (that is, don't lash out in public or inappropriately express your irritability); however, instead of rigidly resisting your anger, you simply let the anger pass without judgment. This still prevents any inappropriate expression of your irritability, but in a much more healthy way. Instead of suppressing your anger because of concerns about how bad that emotion is, you are fostering a nonreactive stance toward it that will enable you to achieve peace and be free from a desire to lash out.

Throughout this book, we will explain how to mindfully regulate your emotions, which can be especially tricky when it comes to anxiety. Because anxiety expresses itself in so many forms—mentally, physically, and behaviorally—managing it requires thoughtful practice and deliberate use of techniques that target the exact causes of anxiety. Moreover, you will find it helpful to understand why these techniques work the way they do. To that end, we will present a set of skills informed by psychological science and theory that have been proven to help people gain mastery over a variety of emotions in different situations.

Why We Wrote This Book

As we will discuss throughout this book, anxiety and fear, in their most basic form, are typically helpful processes that contribute to intelligence, creativity, performance, and even survival. Both anxiety and fear serve evolutionary and functionally helpful purposes, such as helping you build mastery (for example, when you rehearse an upcoming speech over and over until it's nearly perfect), helping you develop social connections with others, and helping you avoid harm. Yet in modern society, anxiety is the most common class of mental health disorders and has significant implications for public health. Currently, approximately one in five adults in the US suffers from a diagnosable anxiety disorder. Americans collectively spend slightly more than $40 billion a year on health care and related costs (medications, hospital/primary care visits, therapy, self-help, and so on), which is around one-third of the total cost of all mental health care services in the country. People with anxiety disorders are three to five times as likely to use health care services as those with no anxiety disorders. Moreover, many are at risk for developing a second anxiety disorder or even a mood disorder, such as depression.

Despite the high rates of anxiety disorders and their staggering economic burden, only about 35 percent of people with a diagnosable anxiety condition are receiving some type of professional mental health treatment. This means that almost two-thirds of Americans who have an anxiety disorder aren't receiving treatment for a host of distressing symptoms that affect their ability to function at home, at work or school, or in social settings. This should serve as a motivation for psychologists and other mental health care professionals to develop innovative ways of decreasing the burden of anxiety disorders. One way is to help people—including those who are in need of treatment for problematic anxiety, those who are already in treatment for problematic anxiety, and those who want to mitigate their risk of developing problematic anxiety—reduce their anxiety symptoms through education-based initiatives grounded in scientific principles. We wrote this book with this very idea in mind.

Whom This Book Is For

This book is for anyone who wants to better manage and ultimately outsmart his or her anxiety. Everyone experiences anxiety at some point, but its effects—meaning the way you feel when you are anxious—vary from person to person. For some people, anxiety might be a mild irritation or a nuisance, whereas for others it can be incredibly distressing or even debilitating. Regardless of where your symptoms fall on this spectrum, you can use this book as a self-directed, empirically based guide for managing everyday symptoms of anxiety. The information and practice suggestions presented throughout this book are intended to help you achieve a meaningful reduction in anxiety by learning to think differently about your anxiety, changing your reactions to your emotions, and acquiring new habits to skillfully confront and outsmart your anxiety. We want to provide you, or anyone you know who's seeking help in managing his or her anxiety, with a comprehensive and integrated daily self-help guide.

This book will also be equally useful for anyone who doesn't have problematic anxiety or a diagnosable condition but who does experience unhelpful or unnecessary anxiety from time to time. In fact, many of the principles and skills in this book can be used by anybody. You certainly don't have to be struggling with anxiety in order to learn mindfulness or to learn better emotion management, but you do have to be committed to learning and practicing the material.

We would encourage all readers to think of their commitment to this book in much the same way as they might make a commitment to improving any other aspect of their life. If you want the body of a world-class athlete, you have to commit to training daily; if you want the intellect of a top scientist, you have to commit to a rigorous course of academic study; and if you want the wealth of a billionaire, you have to commit to developing financial success through smart investments. If you want to retrain your mind (your thoughts and emotions) and your body (the way your body responds to anxiety) in order to enhance your mental health, then it's important that you commit to incorporating into your everyday life the ideas and skills contained in this book.

This book may also be useful for mental health and other health care professionals who work with people who report feeling excessively anxious. Many of the skills taught in this book can easily be adapted for use in psychotherapy or as a complement to professional therapy services. This book, however, is not a substitute for the professional services of a mental health care practitioner, especially if you believe you can't manage your anxiety on your own. If you are already receiving treatment for a psychological condition, we encourage you to discuss and share this book with your therapist or counselor. If you are experiencing thoughts of suicide or self-harm, immediately seek help from a mental health care professional or your primary care physician.

Using This Book to Manage Your Anxiety

This book is one of the first to present an integrated model of mindfulness and emotion regulation. Its purpose is to help you reduce and manage your anxiety symptoms by using interventions that have a scientific basis. Each chapter is based on original yet enduring psychological science, all of which has implications for how you mindfully manage your emotions in an effort to manage your anxious mood. We will present the information in an understandable way, and we will explain how to apply the scientific concepts to your everyday life. Many books talk about how understanding emotions can be helpful or offer tips to reduce anxiety, but this book will explain the strong connection between anxiety and emotions and how regulating your emotions in a mindful way can help you make significant improvements in your everyday life, including your social interactions, your work obligations, and your family responsibilities.

Each chapter presents a series of skills that will help you think and respond differently to your anxiety. Very often, people's habitual ways of dealing with problems or certain situations breed anxiety. On the other hand, some of the habits you have developed to manage your anxiety probably work exceedingly well. When you notice that a particular management strategy works well for you, be sure to note this in a journal or on your mobile device and use that strategy in the future. As for the habits that don't work well for you, we intend to help you break them while also developing skills that will be more helpful and effective in managing your anxiety.

If you truly want to outsmart your anxiety, you will find this book valuable for its examination of various psychological theories on anxiety and their links to emotions and certain automatic ways of thinking. We will teach you how and when to pay attention to your anxiety, how to react with less intensity to your anxious emotions, and what to do when you feel as if you are overwhelmed by anxiety. We will also discuss how to avoid thinking in negative ways, which is an anxiety trap. Later in the book, we will provide an overview of conscious and unconscious processing of information, both of which can contribute to anxiety.

Using the Online Content

The companion website to this book (http://www.newhar binger.com/34169) features audio recordings, worksheets, and more. It will provide you with additional tips and exercises to illustrate concepts and instructions contained in the chapters. You will be able to download mindfulness exercises as audio files for listening purposes or for when you are "on the go." This will help bring the contents of the book to life while you are actively involved in your daily life. Other online content will include forms for tracking your use of skills, tips for using skills in everyday situations, and resources for further exploration.

chapter 1

Linking Anxiety, Emotion, and Mindfulness

Emotions can serve a variety of purposes. They facilitate your attention and direct your behavior in ways that can help you reach your goals. Thus, psychologists say that emotions have *functional* value. For example, if you encounter a skunk while walking outside, your fearful emotional response will not only increase your attention to the skunk, but also likely lead you to slowly back away from it to avoid being sprayed. Scientists have suggested that many emotions, even those that are initially unpleasant—such as anxiety—also have an evolutionary purpose and can be better understood as functional mental processes. Although this claim might be difficult to reconcile with an emotion such as anxiety, it will become more apparent after you learn how our current definition of emotion applies to anxiety itself. By examining each feature of anxiety, you will be in a better position to understand why anxiety prompts you to behave and think the way you do in threatening situations.

What Are Emotions?

Although scientists have invested a great deal of research in studying the underlying nature of emotions, it has been rather difficult for them to specify exactly what the term "emotions" involves. That's because emotions are incredibly broad and complex. Often, people can think of general concepts associated with emotions, such as "feelings" or "moods," or they can list several examples of emotions, such as "joy," "fear," "sadness," and "surprise." However, by failing to identify core characteristics that apply to a wide range of individual emotional states, we all seem to be sidestepping what we really mean by "emotions."

The following exercise may give you some insight and help you identify most of the relevant features of an emotion.

Practice   Close your eyes and recall a situation in which you experienced a very strong emotion, such as happiness or anger. Reflect on what happened immediately before the onset of the emotion—what specific events or interactions contributed to that reaction? Consider what subjective and physical experiences accompanied this emotional state. Focus on what the emotion was guiding you to do. (It's likely that a strong emotion, such as happiness or anger, would encourage you to respond to your emotional experience in some way.)

Klaus Scherer, a distinguished research psychologist, was responsible for a very prominent and widely adopted framework for understanding both the function and nature of emotions. An important aspect of Scherer's *component process model* (Scherer 2005) is that it goes beyond the commonly held belief that emotions amount to nothing more than feelings. Instead, emotions are recognized as a multifaceted process involving *cognitive appraisals, physical symptoms, action tendencies, communicative expression,* and *feelings.*

Imagine you are hiking a trail with your friends when you notice what looks like a snake right in front of you on the path. Initially, this situation requires a *cognitive appraisal,* or a judgment call, to clarify exactly what that snakelike object is. It could be a number of things: a piece of rope, a twisted branch, or an actual snake. Before responding, you need to be able to appraise whether this object is dangerous and warrants any sort of emotional response. Depending on the situation, you may have different thresholds for considering something threatening. It would be inefficient and exhausting to regard absolutely anything remotely scary as a true threat, whereas it could be risky to disregard potential danger and write it off as entirely unlikely. That's why it's especially important to maintain good emotional balance grounded in reality: to accurately identify what's likely to occur.

After you identify the object as a snake, bodily and mental responses emerge to facilitate goal-directed behavior. In other words, *physical symptoms* coincide with subjective *feelings* to communicate important messages regarding the nature of the external stimulus (the snake). These physical symptoms might include a racing heart, sweating, and rapid breathing, which would all contribute to a subjective feeling of fear. Physical symptoms and feelings are sometimes referred to as the "experiential components" of emotions, because they are the classical aspects of emotions that individuals directly experience and perceive. Once these experiences occur, you often don't just sit with them and do nothing. They are there to motivate you to take action! This is what people mean by the "fight-or-flight" response, in which you either confront the danger or flee to safety. These *action tendencies* enable you to respond adaptively to various situations and help you achieve the best outcomes possible under the conditions. For instance, you might determine that the snake is poisonous and that you need to get away. Your fear is like an alarm or warning system for your body. Confronting a true danger, such as a poisonous snake, leaves no time for long, drawn-out deliberation to determine your course of action. You need to react immediately and in a manner that preserves your own welfare. Emotions can stimulate quick and efficient action.

Finally, you might feel inclined to *communicate* your emotional experience and intentions to others. For instance, you might tell your friends that everyone should immediately run from the snake to avoid harm. Or perhaps you might communicate your intention to defend yourself and confront the threat. Such emotional expression, whether verbal or nonverbal, often facilitates and accompanies the action tendency itself. The importance of identifying emotions and relating them to others is evident from an evolutionary perspective. Humans are community-oriented creatures that value emotional expression and communication. Such behaviors foster a greater sense of cohesion and provide others with valuable information regarding the surrounding environment. Thus, emotions ultimately help you and those around you survive and succeed.

The component process model works with just about any type of emotion. No doubt you can easily conceive of how your appraisal of a situation might lead you to feel sadness or happiness and how that sadness or happiness might direct your behavioral responses to help you accomplish relevant goals (for example, to learn how to problem solve in the face of failure or loss). Though clarifying the nature of emotions enables us to have a more fine-grained discussion of anxiety, this is only part of the puzzle. The ability to manage or regulate emotions in a flexible manner proves essential to mental health, and this is our next topic.

Practice   Think of a recent time when you experienced the emotion of disgust. Bring to mind your initial appraisals of the object or situation that made you feel disgusted. Identify the feelings, physical sensations, and action tendencies associated with this experience. As you become comfortable with this exercise, we encourage you to try it again with other emotions.

What Is Emotion Regulation?

As we alluded to above, emotions are purposeful in nature. They can guide and direct you to pursue relevant goals in an efficient manner. However, the relationship between emotions and actions is not just one-way, such that emotions lead to behavior. Rather, you also have the ability to influence your emotional experience. Emotion regulation refers to "the processes by which individuals influence which emotions they have, when they have them, and how they experience and express these emotions" (Gross 1998, 275). Like emotions themselves, emotion regulation is a complex phenomenon that proves difficult to define. Nevertheless, research has identified some core features of emotion regulation that are worth mentioning.

Building on contemporary conceptualizations of emotions, James Gross (1998) developed a very influential theory of emotion regulation, which he called the *process model*. In this model, five different processes unfold over time and contribute to the expression and regulation of emotions. Prior to experiencing emotion, you can make use of a future-oriented process called *situation selection*. In other words, you can consciously choose to participate in certain situations that make pleasant emotions more likely or avoid those that make unpleasant emotions more likely. For instance, have you ever attempted to avoid your boss because being in his presence makes you feel anxious and uncomfortable? By purposefully choosing to avoid him, you make it less likely that you will experience these sorts of negative emotions. Conversely, attempts to spend time with cherished friends might count as forward-looking ways to select situations that produce positive emotions. As you will see later in this book, dysfunctional ways of using situation selection are largely to blame for anxiety and related emotions.

If you can't avoid an anxiety-provoking situation altogether, you can still alter your emotional experience in that situation by way of *situation modification*. In other words, you can still influence how the situation will give rise to emotions as it occurs. Imagine that you are stumbling on most of your words as you deliver a presentation. Obviously, this could be very embarrassing, even petrifying. A mind racing with concerns about what your audience must think of you is enough to create a very unpleasant experience indeed. But imagine that you use humor to defuse the situation. Jesting about your blunders puts everyone at ease and reduces the burden you would normally place on yourself. In this way, making explicit attempts to change the nature of a dreadful situation, instead of simply enduring the situation, can lead to an entirely different emotional experience.

Even if there are no ways to change what's happening, you can still alter your experience of the situation by the way in which you use your *attention*. Directing your focus either away or toward certain features of your current environment enables you to magnify or subdue the intensity of an emotion. Imagine that you are out shopping with your mother and she says something that embarrasses you in front of a clerk. By distracting yourself or moving your attention away from the comments and the clerk's reaction, you can limit the extent to which you experience shame or embarrassment. Moreover, you can use *cognitive appraisals*, or the way in which you think about or assess a situation, to alter your perception of the event and the significance of the emotion. For instance, instead of construing your mother's sensitive comments as anxiety-provoking and humiliating, you might think about the fact that you will likely never see this clerk again. It might not matter very much what he thinks about you, seeing as his opinion won't affect you in the future.

The last process is *response modulation*. Response modulation refers to direct attempts to influence the action tendency produced by the emotion. These attempts can be physical, mental, or behavioral. High levels of anxiety can motivate you to minimize your exposure to a feared situation or person as much as possible. To take the scary boss scenario, if you couldn't avoid an encounter with your frightening boss, your anxiety might compel you to try to keep the conversation short and remove yourself from his presence quickly. The way in which you responded to this avoidance action tendency could influence your overall emotional experience. One option would be to accept your anxiety and desire to avoid your boss but not let these things dictate your eventual action. By exposing yourself to this feared situation, you could alter the way in which you naturally responded to it. Another common example of response modulation is suppression. For example, high levels of anger may prompt you to lash out at whomever or whatever caused your frustration; however, this might not be appropriate in certain situations. If you are in public, yelling or venting may attract unwanted attention and exacerbate the situation. Conscious efforts to suppress or subdue the expression of anger may be required.

Practice   Think of recent times in your life when you regulated your emotions using these different processes (situation selection, situation modification, attention, cognitive appraisals, and response modulation). Consider how you selected and modified your situation, how your interpretation of the situation and use of attention influenced your emotions, and whether you tried to change the course of action your emotions guided you to take.

With these models of emotion and emotion regulation in mind, we devote the remainder of the book to specific ways in which efforts to regulate your emotions can go wrong and how you can overcome these challenges. Successfully regulating your emotions requires careful flexibility and knowing when to use certain strategies. There's a wealth of research on the ways in which certain emotion regulation strategies affect mental health and anxiety. Our integrated account of emotion regulation and mindfulness (our next topic) will enable you to determine under what conditions you should use certain techniques and why these emotion regulation strategies work the way they do.

The Link Between Anxiety and Emotion

In any situation, the emergence of anxiety is preceded by thoughts and beliefs about the situation. In other words, it's your determination that a threat exists that leads you to feel anxiety.

Imagine that you are about to give a speech. Casting your gaze over the audience, you realize that there could be a social cost if you perform poorly. In other words, the fact that you might fail to meet listeners' expectations gives you concern over how you might appear and a fear of negative evaluation. Yet this is only one possible way for you to appraise the situation. Another would be to regard the speech as an enjoyable opportunity to give a performance. That appraisal would likely give rise to far less anxiety. Thus, it's the appraisal of a potential threat that feeds the emergence of full-blown anxiety.

If you perceive giving a speech to be a threatening situation, a series of physical and subjective feelings will ensue. These particular sensations are what people associate most often with anxiety, as they can cause significant discomfort and distress. Anxious emotions bring about rapid heartbeat, constricted breathing, sweating, and general physiological arousal. These symptoms exacerbate subjective feelings of apprehension and dread. As mentioned before, in these situations the flight-or-fight response can become active, which prompts behaviors meant to help you either avoid danger or fend it off. You might feel inclined to adopt various *safety behaviors*. Such behaviors involve attempts to temporarily dampen feelings of anxiety by avoiding whatever seems threatening. Continuing with the example of giving a speech, looking only at your notes throughout the speech might enable you to distract yourself and avoid your audience's scrutinizing gaze. Similarly, you might rush through the speech or end it abruptly so that you escape the perceived threat of the audience. Whether the threat is real or not, your anxiety coordinates various physical and mental systems to enable you to react in such a way as to fend off or flee from possible harm.

What's important to consider in the current context is a key distinction some researchers draw between fear and anxiety: whereas fear is often associated with a specific stimulus that poses an immediate risk, anxiety represents an apprehensive approach toward nonspecific threats that may occur at some uncertain future time. Essentially, anxiety maintains a free-floating sense of dread that something bad might happen without knowing exactly what form it will take and when it might occur. A keyed-up feeling, the feeling of being on your toes, contributes to the high levels of distress inherent in prolonged anxiety. It's true that there are times when sustained levels of anxiety appropriately help people stay alert because something could go wrong at any moment—think of combat situations or insurmountable financial difficulties. Most of the time, however, prolonged anxiety usually doesn't prove especially beneficial, making it important to draw a line between helpful and unhelpful expressions of fear.

Helpful vs. Problematic Emotions

So far, our discussion of emotions and anxiety might seem a bit counterintuitive, because we have been talking about emotions having an adaptive, functional value, yet these are the very phenomena that seem to be causing your problems.

How can emotions be so double-natured? It's true that temporary fear occurring in the context of a menacing animal or a loud noise is the sort of thing that can help you avoid real danger. But some occurrences of dread and apprehension thwart people's efforts to maintain normal, happy lives. Part of the reason for this comes from the distinction we just made between anxiety and fear. Certain manifestations of and responses to emotion, which have a great deal to do with what makes us all human, can interfere with quality of life and cause significant distress.

Human beings possess very complex intellectual and cognitive faculties. One consequence of this is that we are able to assign metaphorical significance to a variety of situations and think in abstract terms about future events. Often, we can "perceive" a possible threat when that threat isn't necessarily forthcoming. It's not as if we are conjuring up monsters, but our minds are designed to be overly cautious in appraising threat. As the saying goes, "Better safe than sorry." Better to plan everything out beforehand and be on guard for a worst-case scenario.

We all know there's uncertainty in the world and in our future, and anxiety is our way of preparing for it. The problem with extreme forms of anxiety is that they encourage you to overestimate the likelihood of a disaster. As we mentioned before, anxiety can lead you to believe that even the most benign situation involves a threat. To return to the example of public speaking, the truth is that more often than not, at least half of your audience wouldn't notice or care about minor blunders and the exact content of whatever you were saying. When you feel "on the spot" to such a great extent that you believe people are scrutinizing and analyzing every aspect of your performance and appearance, however, it can put your mind and body in "defense mode." You perceive a danger or high social cost, which causes more distress and interference than the situation warrants. This anxiety tends to generalize, meaning you tend to later also experience it in other situations and contexts. It extends beyond your immediate and present environment to more general concerns and possible future incidents. This is what makes anxiety problematic.

A common response to uncertainty is worry. When you worry, you are in essence attempting to conceive of a rational solution that will equip you to deal with the unknown. Because one of the core action tendencies accompanying anxiety is avoidance, contemplating over and over again how to handle or avoid some ominous future event can seem necessary. A key feature of worry is that it reflects a negative form of repetitive thinking. Compared to true problem solving, which is a proactive approach to a real concern without an excessively negative focus, worry falls short in many ways. Often when people worry, they do so to avoid the prospect of an unpleasant emotion, but dwelling on what the future may hold actually gets in the way of solving problems and can be completely unproductive. High levels of anxiety can cause you to worry about events that are highly unlikely or to underestimate your ability to cope with disaster, leading you to spend an inordinate amount of time trying to come up with ways of dealing with all the negative possibilities you can imagine.

As a general rule, even emotions that are inherently distressing, such as anxiety, facilitate a variety of helpful behaviors. How you respond to these emotions determines whether they will be helpful or harmful. We have seen how reasonable levels of fear can develop into unproductive, distressing anxiety depending on the approach you take. The future is always uncertain, and thus you might naturally feel concerned about it; however, the decision to use worry versus other approaches can have a major impact on your mental health. This is why it's incredibly important to use good judgment in both your evaluation of threat and your choice of responses to your emotions. Being clear about how you respond to emotions and where difficulties might lie is the first step in figuring out how to outsmart your anxiety.

Assessing Your Anxiety and Emotions

Learning to properly assess your anxiety is a healthy and important first step toward understanding the role anxiety has in your life, including its causes and consequences. Defining and measuring your anxiety symptoms will help you decide how best to address and outsmart your anxiety. To this end, we will provide checklists to help you identify common anxiety symptoms, scales for rating both the intensity of your anxiety and your level of distress, and guidelines for formulating and testing hypotheses about your anxiety symptoms. By using these assessment tools, you will be able to:

- Identify the nature and severity of your anxiety.

- Establish baseline measurements of your symptoms so that you can monitor changes in your anxiety as you incorporate skills from this book into your life.

- Determine realistic goals for managing and outsmarting your anxiety.

The Nature of Anxiety

A key aspect of assessing your anxiety is understanding the nature and experience of your symptoms. "Anxiety" is often an all-encompassing term that describes a mood state characterized by fear, apprehension, and avoidance. However, it's important that you distinguish between fear and anxiety so that you can label your experience properly and guide your behavior accordingly. You may recall that we already discussed these differences earlier in this chapter, but it bears repeating so that you can fully understand how they apply to your life. Again, fear is like an alarm or warning system for your body. Fear is a *present-moment* emotional response that works to facilitate your survival.

If you are walking down the street and you encounter a tiger, you very likely will develop a fear response that will motivate you to take action to protect yourself—to fight the tiger, flee from it, or freeze to avoid detection. Okay, so most likely you will never encounter a tiger, but think about the last time you looked in your rearview mirror and saw red and blue lights flashing from a police vehicle. If you are like most people, you instantly felt a sense of dread (and maybe even doom!), followed by fairly immediate changes in your body, such as increased blood pressure and heart rate, nausea, shallow breathing, or a surge of energy. Fear is what enables you to detect sources of threat, to be alert and focused, and to act quickly and decisively.

Anxiety, as we mentioned, is a *future-oriented* emotional response in which you anticipate upcoming threats. Anxiety is characterized by a chronic sense of threat, apprehension and worry about the future, and bodily tension; anxiety is a mechanism to help you prepare or cope with *upcoming* events because you seek to relieve or reduce the tension from your anxiety by preparing for that future threat. Imagine that your friend arranges for you to go on a blind date one week from today. At first, it might sound like a great opportunity to meet someone new, but as you think about making small talk, where you'll go for the date, and whether you should split the check at dinner, you might begin to feel anxious. As the day draws nearer, you might even obsess over what to wear, how you will feel if the person doesn't show up, or whether you and your date will have a good connection. On the day of the date, you might feel nervous or full of too much energy, you might criticize yourself through negative self-talk, or you might even consider canceling. Your anxiety in this scenario is all future-focused and helps you prepare for the date; however, when your anxiety is excessive or out of control, it quickly becomes problematic because it interferes with your ability to realistically and accurately appraise the actual threat of the situation.

Distinguishing Fear from Anxiety   Indicate whether each of the following scenarios is more characteristic of fear or anxiety.

> You are walking alone at night and you see a man walking toward you. The man is wearing a ski mask. You suddenly feel frightened and notice that your heart is racing. You reach for your phone in case you need to call for help, but your hands are shaky and you drop it. **Fear** or **Anxiety**?

> You have been asked to give a toast at your best friend's wedding, and you feel compelled to accept the request, despite your fear of speaking in public. You put off writing your speech for as long as possible; you persistently worry about being judged by those attending the wedding

reception; and you feel a constant dread. On the day of the wedding, right before the reception, you feel as if you might panic and notice you have hives on your face and upper body. *Fear* or *Anxiety*?

While preparing dinner after a long day of work, you notice a mouse scurry by your feet in the kitchen. After a split second, you realize you have jumped up on the kitchen counter and are screaming rather loudly. Although you no longer see the mouse, you remain on the counter until you can call for help from a neighbor, friend, or family member. *Fear* or *Anxiety*?

For as long as you can remember, you have been a chronic worrier. On any given day, you find it hard to concentrate on your work, you feel restless or full of nervous energy, and you find it increasingly difficult to fall asleep at night. Your symptoms seem to be highly associated with your worries, which are excessively focused on your health, your family's health, your finances, and even the state of the world. *Fear* or *Anxiety*?

Answers: 1. Fear; 2. Anxiety; 3. Fear; 4. Anxiety

The Components of Anxiety

Anxiety generally falls into one of two categories. *Transitory* anxiety is characterized by moments of temporary anxiety, such as in response to an impending event or something in your environment. Imagine an Olympic athlete who, moments before his or her name is called or even days before the games begin, experiences intense anxiety due to the enormous pressure of the event.

Dispositional anxiety, on the other hand, is a characteristic way of responding to anxiety-inducing, stressful situations. A person with dispositional anxiety might be prone to experiencing anxiety in multiple areas of his or her life. For example, a person with dispositional anxiety might often feel restless or nervous, worry too much, and have difficulty making decisions at work, at school, at home, and in social interactions.

Anxiety can further be measured according to its intensity and severity. Many mental health care professionals consider anxiety to exist on a spectrum, with symptoms ranging from mild to severe. Imagine that your good friend, who has a fear of flying, has an upcoming trip mandated by work. Your friend's anxiety reaction will be either enhanced or diminished depending on his or her initial level of fear. If your friend has only a slight fear of flying, he or she may experience slight tension, vague restlessness, and some intermittent worries about landing safely. Severe anxiety, on the other hand, might lead your friend to feel intense distress. Your friend may have a full-blown panic attack, attempt to exit the plane before takeoff, drink heavily before boarding to try to cope with the trip, or even plan to avoid flying altogether. Essentially, your level of anxiety, which is informed by how you *think and feel* about the situation (for example, *Airplanes are dangerous; therefore, I must avoid them at all costs or I will feel too anxious or die!*), affects the degree to which you experience distressing symptoms. The amount of distress you experience directly relates to both the intensity and the severity of your symptoms.

The following exercise (available for download at the website for this book) will help you track symptoms of anxiety that may manifest in all kinds of situations and help you examine how those symptoms affect your experiences. Review the following list of common symptoms of anxiety and then indicate how intensely you experienced each symptom in the past month.

Symptoms of Anxiety over the Past Month

Symptom	Intensity			
	None	Mild	Moderate	Severe
Restlessness, surge of energy, or inability to relax	☐	☐	☐	☐
Dizziness or light-headedness	☐	☐	☐	☐
Feeling of terror or fright	☐	☐	☐	☐
Rapid heartbeat or pounding pulse	☐	☐	☐	☐
Fearing the worst, or a foreboding feeling	☐	☐	☐	☐
Trembling, shaking, or weakness	☐	☐	☐	☐
Overestimation of danger	☐	☐	☐	☐
Sweating (not due to heat or exertion)	☐	☐	☐	☐
Excessive and uncontrollable worry	☐	☐	☐	☐
Rapid or shallow breathing	☐	☐	☐	☐

Don't Let Anxiety Run Your Life

Anxiety is multifaceted, meaning its symptoms are wide-ranging and manifest differently depending on the person, the type of anxiety, and the context in which it occurs. As you can tell from the preceding list, there are many symptoms of anxiety, and they can arise either separately or in combination, at any time, and for no discernible reason! To illustrate this, imagine a group of kindergarteners who are going to a petting zoo. On the way there, all of them are excited. Once they arrive at the petting zoo, however, many of the children will have entirely different reactions—including different thoughts, emotions, behaviors, and physiological reactions—to the prospect of petting the various animals. Some will remain excited and pet each animal they encounter, some will be apprehensive and may only poke or touch a few animals, and others will outright avoid most, if not all, of the animals. This latter group of children will very likely experience anxiety in their body, overestimate the dangers involved in touching the animals, feel frightened and sheepish (no pun intended), or exhibit obstinate behaviors. When we consider why these children might be anxious, it's important to think about the various factors that lead them to feel anxious *and* to what degree. For example, genetics, gender, personality, prior learning experiences, emotional experiences, physical symptoms, thoughts, and many other factors all influence how a person will uniquely react to his or her environment.

To more closely examine how anxiety affects your experiences, let's consider the various facets of anxiety. Using the following checklist, place a check mark in the box on the left if you have experienced each symptom at least once in your lifetime. Then, place a check mark in the box on the right if it tends to be an ongoing problem for you.

Symptoms of Anxiety over Your Lifetime

Occasional	Symptom	Persistent
☐	Unreasonable fear of an object (such as animals or blood) or a situation (such as flying or heights)	☐
☐	Marked fear or anxiety about social situations in which you might be exposed to scrutiny or judgment	☐
☐	Unexpected panic during which you are overcome by sudden intense fear or discomfort for no apparent reason	☐
☐	Excessive anxiety and worry, for at least six months, about a number of events or activities	☐
☐	Experiencing or witnessing a life-threatening or traumatic event involving serious injury or death	☐
☐	Inappropriate thoughts, impulses, or images that you can't get out of your mind, such as preoccupation with germs or sexual impulses	☐
☐	Spending more than one hour a day doing repetitive and unproductive actions, such as hand-washing, checking, or counting	☐
☐	Fear and avoidance of places or situations that you perceive to be dangerous, uncomfortable, or unsafe and that might cause you to panic and make you feel trapped, helpless, or embarrassed	☐

Anxiety and Emotions and Their Relationships to Mindfulness

If you have ever spent time at the beach, you are probably well aware that ocean waves not only differ in size and shape but also move with varying speed and intensity. That's part of the fun of swimming in the ocean! Thanks to modern forecasting, ocean currents are generally predictable, but of course, conditions can change with little notice. The calm and soothing ocean can quickly become vicious and destructive, depending on conditions of the water itself, such as thermal patterns, and conditions outside of the water, such as the wind and the weather. Emotions are very much like waves and can easily influence the way you think, act, and respond to various situations in your life. Emotions, again much like the ocean, can also be affected by internal (physiological) and external (environmental) conditions. Most of the time, your emotions are quite predictable and manageable, but every now and then, like a big ocean wave, they can get the best of you!

Rate the Intensity of Your Emotions   Take a moment to review the following list of basic human emotions. Then, for each one, identify a time during the last week (or the last several weeks) when you experienced this emotion. Next, rate the intensity with which you felt the emotion by comparing it to ocean waves on a scale of 1 to 5, where 1 = small waves and 5 = large surfing waves.

Basic Emotion	Situation	Wave Intensity Rating (1–5)
Happiness		
Sadness		
Anger		
Fear		
Excitement		
Disgust		

As we have discussed, fear and anxiety, at their core, are emotions. These emotions, along with many others, serve useful functions. As you might guess from what you have already read, fear and anxiety serve to motivate your behavior (immediate or long term), communicate to others how you are feeling, and even help you better understand an uncertain situation. Emotions are adaptive in that they guide you toward a more balanced sense of self and a better quality of life.

Like any emotion, however, fear or anxiety can quickly become problematic and overwhelming. Many symptoms of anxiety result from reactive, judgmental, and inflexible responses to negative emotions. When these occur, it's often helpful to consider how you will manage your emotions so that they once again serve a useful function, rather than create problems for you.

As we have discussed, emotion regulation will help you flexibly manage the intensity of your emotions by lessening, maintaining, or increasing the intensity of your emotional reactions (Gross 1998; Davidson 2010). Imagine that you have to take an exam at work. For some people, taking an exam might evoke a great deal of anxiety; others may feel apathetic about the entire process. Your reaction will depend on what the exam means to you. For example, is your performance on the exam important to obtaining a promotion, or is it ultimately inconsequential? Depending on your reaction to having to take an exam, you may have to lessen or increase the intensity of your emotional state so that you can adequately prepare for it.

Practice   Think of recent times in your life when you purposely had to lessen, maintain, or increase the intensity of your emotional reaction. For example, the last time you felt sad, did you do something to adjust the amount of sadness you were feeling? Similarly, the last time you felt overly anxious, what did you do, if anything, to manage your anxiety? Sometimes people avoid thinking about what's causing the emotion by distracting themselves, denying their experience, or focusing more on their symptoms of anxiety than on what's actually causing them to feel anxious. By thinking about ways to manage the intensity of your emotions, you can identify those strategies that have been helpful and those that have been unhelpful in changing your emotional experiences.

The concept of emotion regulation has been increasingly investigated in the last decade, and this work has important implications for advancing theories on why anxiety symptoms develop and the severity of their manifestation. Fear and anxiety are distinct emotions that require people to purposefully exert some control over them, especially when the fear or anxiety is excessive or causing dysfunction in everyday life. Clinical research demonstrates that emotion regulation can either augment or diminish fear and anxiety, depending on the type of emotion regulation strategy a person employs.

Mindfulness is a key component of helping you regulate your emotions, especially when you are anxious. Mindfulness entails "paying attention in a particular way, on purpose, in the present moment, and nonjudgmentally" (Kabat-Zinn 1994, 4). According to research, an important benefit of mindfulness is the ability to shift or transform your perspective by distancing yourself from your emotional experiences (Herbert and Forman 2011). In other words, mindfulness entails, at least in part, learning to observe your emotions— rather than identifying with them—without criticism or judgment and with compassion. In practice, when an emotion arises, mindfulness allows you to notice it with curiosity rather than immediately and reflexively react to it. The same is true when several emotions occur all at once or in waves. With mindfulness, your emotions will become more predictable, manageable, and adaptive.

What Does Mindfulness Entail?

In addition to the definitions of mindfulness mentioned above, empirically informed theories of mindfulness have been developed. The one we focus on here is derived, in part, from our own recent research (Curtiss and Klemanski

2014a). There has been increasing consensus that mindfulness is multifaceted and that different components of mindfulness serve different functions. One conceptualization theorizes that there are five factors of mindfulness: observation, acting with awareness, describing, nonjudgment, and nonreactivity (Baer et al. 2006). Though distinct, these factors interact in such a way as to give rise to overall mindfulness.

Observation refers to the basic attentional processes you use to focus on your environment. This becomes important in the overall context of *acting with awareness,* or using your attention to focus on the present moment and behaving in such a way that reflects your present awareness. Common mindfulness exercises encourage you to focus on various aspects of your present environment. The goal of these exercises is for you to not be distracted by thoughts regarding the past or future, developing a type of concentration that will eventually enable you to "just be" and experience consciousness of all the internal and external experiences that arise. Such fine-grained focus allows you to be equally precise in your *description* of your experience. By distinguishing various aspects of your experience with different verbal labels, you can better focus your present awareness and appreciate the diverse nature of your overall experience.

Such present-centered awareness is accomplished in a certain way, namely *nonjudgmentally* and *nonreactively.* Whenever you mindfully direct your attention to various aspects of your environment, you don't evaluate your thoughts and experience. Rather, you let the contents of your subjective mental world pass through your mind without reacting to them.

A key aspect of mindfulness is that none of these components (observation, acting with awareness, describing, nonjudgment, or nonreactivity) is sufficient by itself. Observation alone, for example, doesn't quite contribute to mindfulness (Desrosiers et al. 2014). Observation needs to be coupled with a nonjudgmental and nonreactive disposition. Furthermore, embracing mindfulness promotes the cultivation of two related mental processes: decentering and acceptance. *Decentering* entails achieving psychological distance from your thoughts, your emotions, and the surrounding environment, and is critical to emotion regulation. Instead of placing a great deal of importance on worrisome thoughts about his or her performance during a speech, for example, a person who uses mindfulness to decenter may appreciate that these thoughts can pop up without any consequence or need for judgment. Moreover, this leads to *acceptance* of emotional states, or not feeling a strong urge to control and react to them (Hayes et al. 2006). Trying to integrate into your daily life all of these components at once can certainly be difficult! For that reason, the skills presented in this book will build on one another. Little by little, we will present various exercises that will enable you to foster mindfulness and mental equanimity.

chapter 2

Overcoming Attention Biases

During most of your daily activities, various emotions and feelings grab or compete for your attention. For instance, as you prepare to go to work in the morning, you might focus on the stress involved in being on time, or you might worry about being ready to deal with upcoming tasks. Attending a social gathering might elicit feelings of anxiety and fear about how others perceive you.

Whenever strong emotions emerge, it's natural to want to pay attention to them. Paying attention to your emotions seems like a good idea. It gives you an opportunity to analyze, understand, and identify your thoughts and feelings. However, the consequences of a close inspection of your emotions depend on *how* you attend to them. Some forms of attention can be quite harmful, leading to more anxiety and an inability to "get out of your head." Paying attention to your emotions in a *nonjudgmental* and *nonreactive* manner, on the other hand, enables you to achieve a critical distance from negative thoughts. This is the basis of mindfulness, which refers to paying attention to the present moment without judgment or reaction. In this chapter, we will teach you how to reduce your judgments and how to be less reactive to your emotions by engaging in mindfulness-based practices.

Attention and Observation

Imagine the following scenario. Right after you arrive at work one morning, your supervisor requests that you give everyone a thirty-minute presentation about your team's recent progress on several projects. You politely agree, but inside you feel frantic and panicky. Worries about feeling underprepared and concerns about how your coworkers might evaluate you consume your mind. Indeed, you notice that your heart begins to race, your palms feel sweaty, and your chest feels tight. Rather than focus on the task at hand by organizing necessary materials for the presentation, you anticipate the ways in which you might seem like a failure in the eyes of your coworkers and your supervisor. During the presentation itself, maintaining your focus on the content of your talk becomes nearly impossible, as most of your attention is on your emotions and your physical symptoms of anxiety. Furthermore, you are doing more than merely attending to your emotions throughout this ordeal. You are doing it in a certain way. Focusing on your fear of how others perceive you is inevitably accompanied by *judgments* and *evaluations* of what these emotions mean. Judging the presence of fear as bad or as a sign that you are not in control of your feelings leads you to believe that you are inadequate or that you lack the ability to accomplish the task at hand. In other words, these judgments make you equate how you feel with who you really are. The need to evaluate your actions and feelings according to certain standards causes you distress because you don't think you are able to meet those standards.

This judgmental stance toward your internal thoughts inevitably gives rise to a variety of responses and reactions. During your presentation, judging your fear as bad or something negative leads you to attempt to rigidly control or hide your emotions. Second-order reactions, or reactions that you have in response to your initial emotions, cause you to get stuck or fixated on your current experience, thereby preventing you from attending freely to the present moment. Reactive thoughts prevent you from "getting out of your head," as you continue to dwell on your current circumstances. The need to react to your emotions stems from a belief that certain emotions are undesirable or that they may be harmful to your moment-to-moment experiences.

The important thing to note about adopting a judgmental and reactive approach toward negative feelings, such as anxiety, is that it does more harm than good. It prevents you from accomplishing your goals, and it leads to excessive distress. To further clarify the importance of *how* paying attention to your emotions influences your overall anxiety, it's important that we distinguish between helpful and harmful forms of attention.

The ability to observe your thoughts and emotions is a defining human characteristic. The meaning you attach to your observations of your thoughts and emotions shapes your subjective experience to a great degree. Imagine that one of your friends drags you to a social engagement attended by people you have never met. Although your friend assures you that she will stay by your side the whole time, she ends up leaving you alone. Negotiating these sorts of social situations can be especially tough, because it's easy to create an imaginary divide between you and the rest of the attendees. It might be nerve-wracking to join in a conversation among a small group of people or to introduce yourself to a single person hovering over the food. You might worry about what people will think of you, how well you will present yourself, or whether you will find entertaining things to say. Even with this heavy load on your shoulders, by fostering mindfulness as a skillful approach to managing your emotions, you can alter the way you attend to these issues and achieve lasting relief from anxiety.

Imagine that at this social engagement, you decide to start a conversation with a woman whom you have never met. You are worried that you don't know what to say and worried about how she will react; however, there's no need to identify yourself with these worries. You can allow negative thoughts, such as *She will think I'm an idiot because I don't know what to talk about* and *She will know I'm anxious because my heart is racing a mile a minute,* to pass. After all, they are just thoughts. These unhelpful thoughts don't have to affect your perception of yourself *unless you choose to evaluate them in a certain way.* In other words, not judging negative thoughts as a reflection of yourself can transform your outlook from anxious to optimistic. By refraining from making evaluations about what your thoughts must reveal about you as a person, you will have a better chance of meeting your goal: engaging this person in conversation.

Moreover, a judgment-free approach enables you to let go of the need to react. Your pounding heart (or any physical symptom of anxiety) becomes problematic only if you *judge* it to be a disastrous symptom that proves you are too anxious to successfully negotiate the social situation. By not thinking of it as such, you won't feel a strong need to react to these sensations (for example, by crossing your arms to "hide" physical symptoms of anxiety or taking deep breaths to slow your heartbeat). The perceived need to react to anxious thoughts or bodily sensations convinces you that there's a threat or that you must be in total control of yourself to be successful, which isn't true.

Adopting a nonreactive stance by letting go of the need to react to negative thoughts or to be in control of a racing heart enables you to devote your attention to more relevant things, such as the actual conversation you are having with this new acquaintance. The basic idea behind the mindful approach toward attention is that a *nonjudgmental* and *nonreactive* way of perceiving anxiety-provoking experiences prevents you from confirming unhelpful beliefs about your own abilities and the presence of a threat. Figure 2.1 illustrates a basic model of mindful attention that embodies many of the concepts we have discussed so far.

When we consider the impact of attention on symptoms of anxiety, we must acknowledge the importance of two factors: (a) *under what conditions* attention negatively influences anxiety and (b) *how* attention causes changes in anxiety. The former concept we have discussed already: when people are overly reactive toward internal and external experiences, their anxiety and tension increase. But how does this occur? What processes are responsible for the effect of attention on distress? Figure 2.1 provides a framework for answering these questions.

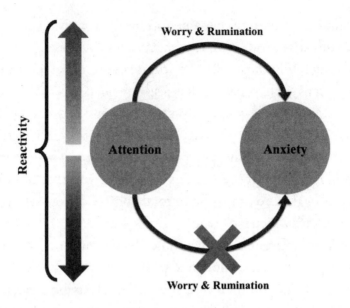

Figure 2.1. Under What Conditions and How Attention Causes Anxiety

In a psychological study (see Desrosiers et al. 2014), we and our colleagues examined various emotion regulation strategies to determine whether they might be responsible for the attention–anxiety relationship. We identified several important processes, including worry and rumination. Although we will describe each of these in further detail in later chapters, it's important for now to note that people use both worry and rumination to try to control or manage unwanted emotions.

Worry may seem to be a useful problem-solving strategy, but it is in fact self-defeating. Worrying excessively about future uncertainties or distressful circumstances often results in greater anxiety and suffering (Borkovec, Ray, and Stöber 1998). Rumination entails repetitive, self-reflective thought about the causes and consequences of emotional distress (Nolen-Hoeksema, Wisco, and Lyubomirsky 2008).

Whereas worry tends to be oriented toward future threats, rumination tends to focus on past experiences. Just like worry, however, prolonged rumination often results in more anxiety.

As figure 2.1 shows, when people are highly reactive to their thoughts and circumstances, increases in attention lead to greater worry and rumination, which eventually result in higher levels of anxiety. The figure also shows that when people *don't* feel a strong need to be reactive, increases in attention aren't related to the use of worry and rumination, thereby reducing overall levels of distress. Let's consider how this model applies to your everyday life.

If you suddenly realize that the deadline for a difficult work project is sooner than you thought it was, you might feel a sense of distress. Your mind might bombard you with negative thoughts and worries (for example, *The project will probably fail because of me, Something will go wrong, and everyone will be disappointed in me,* and *I'm going to get fired.*). By cultivating a nonreactive stance toward these anxiety-provoking thoughts, however—specifically, by leaving each thought as it is and accepting it as something that doesn't require an immediate response—you will be less likely to feel the need to worry about every little detail of the project. Moreover, the emotional distance nonreactivity creates will help you refrain from dwelling on the meaning of past events (such as how you ended up in this situation) and the negative feelings they arouse.

In the rest of this chapter, we will explore the role of attention in anxiety in greater detail. We will also describe the first skill for outsmarting your anxiety and provide detailed instructions and exercises that will help you more mindfully attend to your anxious feelings.

How Anxiety Demands Your Attention

Complex emotions, like anxiety, can be difficult to understand and manage. One way to make sense of your emotions is to look at their function—that is, the purpose they serve. This aids in understanding not only how your everyday emotions can be helpful but also how they can be detrimental to your daily functioning and well-being. Emotions like anxiety can serve to direct your attention to relevant facts and circumstances in the world; however, sometimes this can get out of hand. Examining this function of your anxiety can help you improve how you *judge* and *respond* to anxiety-provoking situations—whether at home, at school, or at work.

Although people often associate anxiety with fear or dread, anxiety can be a helpful experience that contributes to intelligence, creativity, performance, and even survival. It also helps people build mastery or avoid harm. These are all positive functions of anxiety. If you were scheduled to perform at a concert recital or compete in an athletic event, your anxiety would very likely be helpful in terms of motivating you to practice and rehearse so that you could perform at your very best. Other times, however, depending on how you judge or react to your anxiety, it can be less helpful or outright unhelpful. Imagine that you are trying to study for an important exam. Despite your best efforts, anxious thoughts—in the form of fears and worries about not passing the test—intrude and interfere with your concentration and studying. This anxiety is unhelpful because it interferes with your overall goal of doing well on the test. This example illustrates the notion that people who are highly anxious tend to have difficulty attending to their environment and controlling their anxious thoughts. Other unhelpful ways of responding to anxiety include experiencing negative secondary emotions (such as feeling insecure, mistrustful, or frustrated); additional negative thoughts about the situation (for example, *I'm going to make a fool of myself* or *I'm certain I will never be successful in life*); or even unpleasant bodily sensations (such as a racing heart, breathing difficulties, or even a sense of impending doom).

A primary and important function of anxiety is to detect threats in your environment so that you can react accordingly (much as an air traffic controller uses radar to detect threats in the sky or at the airport to avoid danger). By coordinating attention and related cognitive processes, anxiety helps you interact with your surroundings in an efficient and seamless manner. For example, if you are asleep in bed and suddenly wake up to the sound of glass breaking, your anxiety signals that you should investigate the cause of the noise, hide, or leave your house. If you didn't experience such anxiety, you would be more susceptible to harm (imagine ignoring the noise and going back to sleep while a thief burgles your home). Thus, from a functional perspective, anxiety often helps you react by coordinating your thoughts, emotions, and behaviors and by preparing and motivating you to take action (by triggering your fight-or-flight response).

Consider the last time you were asked to do something that made you feel apprehensive or downright anxious. Or think about the last time you had to make small talk with a stranger, prepare for a date, give a speech at work or school, or interact with a police officer. For making small talk or preparing for a date, anxiety may function as a way to detect threat related to rejection, whereas for giving a speech or interacting with a person of authority, anxiety may function as a way to detect threat related to fear of negative evaluation.

Practice   Using an example from your own life, try to identify the function of your anxiety, keeping in mind that anxiety occurs in multiple situations and contexts. What was the threat that you were trying to detect?

Sometimes anxiety occurs even when it's not warranted. For example, sometimes you might *feel* as if you've encountered a bear or as if there's a burglar in your house, but in actuality, there's no bear or burglar or even any apparent reason for your anxious feelings. One key explanation for *how* this occurs is the way anxious individuals pay attention to their environment.

Imagine that when you were a young child, a neighbor's aggressive dog bit you. Ever since then, you have gone out of your way to avoid dogs, and you are often watchful and on guard for the presence of dogs. Perhaps you startle easily when you hear a dog bark on TV, or you are excessively vigilant while walking around your neighborhood in case a dog is running free. To a degree, this is a smart way to guard against harm from dogs, yet because you are prone to view dogs as threats, you tend to pay more attention to anything that might indicate their presence (at the expense of enjoying your walk or other pleasurable activities that you might avoid because of your fear of dogs). This includes not only stimuli related to dogs (such as a "Beware of Dog" sign and the telltale jingle of the tags on a dog's collar) but also unrelated or misperceived stimuli, such as when you mistake a cat or a ball for a small dog or you avoid walking by a certain house because you think you remember seeing a dog there. In this instance, your anxiety is disproportionate to the situation that elicited your anxiety and is likely harmful to your daily functioning or your overall well-being because it's often unwarranted.

Attentional Bias Toward Threat

To facilitate survival, humans have evolved to swiftly respond to threatening stimuli. We even prioritize our attention to threatening stimuli, giving it rapid and dedicated processing in various key parts of our brain. If you were to encounter a bear in the street, your brain would prioritize the bear's presence, which would allow you to act swiftly (and appropriately) to avoid being attacked. Your anxiety would be both warranted and helpful in this situation, but only because you chose to pay attention to the bear and your anxious feelings. If you experience problematic or *maladaptive* anxiety, however, you tend to feel and act as if you are constantly in the presence of a bear (or *could be* in the presence of a bear at any time), with a more generalized, chronic, and pervasive sense of threat.

To illustrate this effect, research psychologists have conducted scientific experiments to better understand *how* attention causes changes in anxiety. Specifically, researchers measured both the speed and the rate of detection of threatening stimuli among anxious versus nonanxious people. One such experiment required participants to scan a number of faces in photographs to detect the "odd man out." There was one angry face among eleven happy faces, for example. Findings from these studies demonstrated that people characterized as highly anxious were faster at detecting the angry face when compared with people who had low or no anxiety. In a different experiment, people who were highly anxious were slower at detecting a neutral face among a number of angry faces (Hansen and Hansen 1988; Byrne and Eysenck 1995; Gilboa-Schechtman, Foa, and Amir 1999; Öhman and Mineka 2001). Other studies, such as the emotional Stroop task, required participants to name the color of ink of various words printed on cards. It sounds easy enough, right? The catch is, the words were emotionally negative ("failure," "collapse," "stupid," "death," and others) and meant to distract from the central task at hand—simply naming a color of ink. Highly anxious people were indeed distracted by the emotionally negative words and displayed more difficulty in correctly naming the ink color than did those with low levels of anxiety or no anxiety (Becker et al. 2001; Dresler et al. 2009).

These experiments highlight two important concepts. First, highly anxious individuals are often, sometimes even without being aware of it, on "high alert" to detect possible threats in their environment. Second, anxious individuals find it hard to focus on a task in the presence of possible threats (Rinck et al. 2003; cf. meta-analysis by Bar-Haim et al. 2007). Further complicating the matter are the ways in which individuals *judge* and *respond* to the thoughts and emotions they have about these enhanced perceptions of threat and increased distractibility. Over time, this process can potentially lead to chronic and debilitating anxiety.

Practice   You may remember that not too long ago, we asked you to consider a particularly anxiety-provoking event and identify the function of your anxiety. With that same event in mind, take a moment to consider how your attentional biases (your tendency to pay more attention to certain types of emotionally threatening stimuli) maintain your anxiety over time. This might entail thinking nonjudgmentally about how you are often on "high alert," either for a specific threat or for many types of threats, or even for threats that aren't actually present or fully real yet. To help you with this exercise, consider the following three interrelated questions:

1. What threats in your environment do you detect more quickly and pay greater attention to? For example, if you tend to worry about never achieving your ambitions, perhaps you pay greater attention to threats of failure or threats to your personal sense of self-worth.

2. What threats, once you notice them, are harder to stop thinking about when compared to others? Do some threats activate your anxiety more than others, such as thinking that a physical symptom means impending doom or that you have a terrible disease?

3. What threats do you purposefully avoid thinking about? Perhaps losing a parent or a child is one of your biggest fears, so you actively avoid thinking about any threats to your family's safety and well-being.

Now, take a moment to consider the ways in which these threats might distract you from everyday moments at home, work, or school.

Attentional Bias Toward Interoceptive Awareness

You tend to know whenever you are anxious, based on clues from your thoughts and emotions. Your body is also a source of information about your level of anxiety. People with anxiety tend to be especially sensitive to their own physical symptoms of anxiety, such as increased heart rate, shallow breathing, and profuse sweating. This type of body sensitivity is known as *interoceptive awareness*, which is another type of attentional bias that's characteristic of people with anxiety, such as those who have panic disorder or generalized anxiety disorder. In essence, anxious people, on average, tend to pay more attention to their bodily sensations and have a lower threshold for interpreting physical signs as problematic or even dangerous.

In several psychological studies, individuals with anxiety disorders were found to have a higher degree of interoceptive awareness (Ehlers and Clark 2000; Van der Does et al. 2000; Pineles and Mineka 2005; Wald and Taylor 2005; White et al. 2006). Other studies have shown that many people with anxiety disorders have higher physiological reactivity (Friedman and Thayer 1998; Lundh and Sperling 2002; Amrhein et al. 2005), especially in response to anxiety-producing stimuli. This means that anxiety disorders, such as social anxiety disorder and post-traumatic stress disorder, tend to be characterized by higher than normal physiological reactivity, among other symptoms. This heightened arousal predisposes people to experience emotions more intensely and to detect potential threats in their environment (for example, someone with anxiety might be more likely to pay attention to something that looks like a scary spider). In fact, heightened interoceptive awareness can lead to increases in anxiety.

During periods of anxiety, most people are prone to pay attention to (in addition to their emotions and thoughts) physical symptoms of anxiety produced by the *autonomic nervous system*, a part of the body that controls the fight-or-flight response. During times of stress, your *sympathetic nervous system*, which is part of the autonomic nervous system, initiates changes in your heart rate, digestion, respiratory rate, pupillary response, and urination. It's quite a useful physiological process, one that prepares you to either flee from a threat or fight it. This process is what helps you (hopefully!) escape when you encounter a bear, but the same process is what can make you feel anxious for no obvious reason.

What do you think your response might be if you actually encountered a bear on the streets of your neighborhood? You might choose to flee from the bear, but you also might freeze or choose to fight it. Your response to this hypothetical situation relates back to how you *judge* and *evaluate* your emotions and how you *react* and *respond* to your thoughts. Your accelerated heart rate and rapid breathing can be a good indicator that the bear is dangerous, and these physical symptoms indicate that you should flee to make yourself safe. Having this kind of interoceptive awareness is perfectly helpful in modulating your reaction to something that's actually a threat (such as a bear!), but it may be out of place in situations that aren't so dangerous (such as giving a speech). By taking your emotions at face value or responding reflexively to every thought, you are not mindfully regulating your emotions. It's important to fine-tune your emotions so that they are appropriate to the severity of a given situation. By reacting to public speaking in the same way as you would react to a bear, you are forgetting to respond to your emotions flexibly. Mindfulness is key to emotional flexibility!

The Mindful Way of Paying Attention

One of the keys to fostering inner peace and outsmarting your anxiety is to use your attention and observational skills adaptively. As mentioned before, you can direct your attention to many features of your environment, both positive and negative. More often than not, people who struggle with stress and anxiety tend to focus on potential threats, which can intensify their initial symptoms of anxiety.

Whenever you realize that your attention is directed toward negative aspects of your life or environment, you have several options, and it's important to distinguish which techniques come from a mindfulness framework and which ones don't. One option is to focus on other aspects of your life or environment, which are perhaps more positive. That is, you can employ distraction as a strategy for reducing the distress associated with attending to things that feel threatening. Though this technique certainly has intuitive appeal, research (for example, Nolen-Hoeksema, Wisco, and Lyubomirsky 2008) has been somewhat inconsistent regarding its effectiveness. It has been suggested that distraction can be used in multiple ways, some more helpful than others. For instance, you can attempt to avoid distress and negative thoughts by preoccupying yourself with several superficial tasks, quickly transitioning from one activity to another—you might decide to watch TV for a few minutes, then read part of a newspaper, then surf the web. Alternatively, you might focus all of your attention on a single task or hobby—for example, you might spend several hours gardening or completing an engrossing puzzle. The former type of distraction is thought to yield little advantage, whereas the latter might promote reductions in stress. Irrespective of how you distract yourself, however, distraction doesn't constitute a form of mindfulness per se. As described earlier, mindfulness techniques focus on changing your *relationship* to internal thoughts rather than changing the *content* of your thoughts. Using distraction doesn't necessarily teach you how to confront your emotions. Instead, it encourages you to alter *what* you are thinking about in the first place. Therefore, distraction certainly can be helpful, but we don't advocate using it often or long term.

A mindful approach to attention requires you to cultivate a nonjudgmental and nonreactive stance toward your emotions. The negative emotion itself can still be present in your mind. In other words, you are being asked not to avoid thinking about unwanted thoughts and distress, but rather to change your relationship to such mental events. As figure 2.1 indicates, observation of your fear and your physical symptoms of anxiety can lead you to try to control your emotions by engaging in negative, repetitive thinking strategies such as worry and rumination. These strategies, however, result in heightened anxiety and might confirm self-defeating beliefs that you are unable to handle scary situations. When you pay attention to your thoughts, emotions, and bodily sensations in a nonreactive manner, you will worry and ruminate less often.

Though this will be explained in greater detail in the next section, nonjudgmental and nonreactive attention comprises a number of important features. The first is that there's no great need for you to distract yourself from negative thoughts. It's fine for you to accept random negative thoughts as a part of normal mental phenomena that require no further action on your part. Second, whenever negative thoughts surface, there's no need to regard them as important signs or as conveying some special meaning about you. So if, during a social interaction, you are suddenly concerned about the meaning of your sweaty palms, you can remember that it would be incorrect to interpret physical symptoms of anxiety as proof that you are unable to successfully negotiate this social situation or that people will perceive you in a negative light. Finally, negative thoughts, such as concern about the meaning of your sweaty palms, don't necessitate a response. They are simply part of the normal course of events that constitutes your mental life. You can just let them be, and they will pass. Fostering this mindful approach toward attention will diminish the likelihood that you will engage in worry and rumination.

Outsmarting Anxiety with Skills Development and Practice

As we have discussed throughout this chapter, it's important for you to pay attention to your emotions, but *how* you do this will be key to better modulating and outsmarting your anxiety. To adopt both a *nonjudgmental* and a *nonreactive* stance toward your emotions, we encourage the use of mindfulness.

As discussed in chapter 1, mindfulness is often referred to as a psychological state of awareness that entails paying attention in a particular way, on purpose, in the present moment, and without judgment or reaction (Kabat-Zinn 1994). It's characterized as a nonjudgmental and nonreactive form of attention to your present-moment experiences, such as your emotions, your thoughts, your bodily sensations, and aspects of your environment.

Mindfulness has been well established as a valuable practice. Many research psychologists have found that mindfulness can help transform both your perspective and your relationship to your emotional experiences. This occurs in two ways:

- Mindfulness serves as an intentional way of self-regulating your attention so that you remain focused on your present-moment experiences, including emotions and related thoughts.

- It cultivates an attitude of openness and acceptance to whatever arises in the present moment (Bishop et al. 2004).

Ultimately, mindfulness will allow you to work toward reducing your anxiety *and* achieving a critical distance from your emotions and thoughts that foster anxiety.

Mindfulness is a skill that you can learn through regular, purposeful practice. By developing or enhancing your mindfulness skills, you can become more open, more accepting, more objective, less judgmental, and less reactive toward your daily experiences. This, in turn, will help reduce your anxiety and allow you to more consistently employ a state of mindful awareness across situations in your everyday life. Indeed, many psychological studies indicate that mindfulness is a healthy way of regulating anxiety and other potentially problematic mood states. For example, as your use of mindfulness increases, your levels of worry and rumination will decrease (Corcoran et al. 2010). Mindfulness is also positively related to effective emotion regulation, suggesting that people who are more mindful also tend to be more successful at regulating their emotional states (rather than feeling controlled by their emotions; Chambers, Lo, and Allen 2008; Teper, Segal, and Inzlicht 2013).

Learning mindfulness can be a lot like learning a new language or practicing for an athletic competition. The more effort you put into practicing mindfulness skills, the better able you will be to notice what reactions you are having and how to flexibly and skillfully attend to situations in your life. If you simply do the suggested practices in this book one time and then forget about them, mindfulness probably won't improve your life very much. Instead, mindfulness is something that you should strive to incorporate into your life so that you can more fully attend to your everyday experiences and reduce your anxiety. With benefits including decreased stress, a better quality of life, improved attention, healthier emotional management, and increased pleasure in daily activities, mindfulness can enhance your everyday life, even above and beyond reducing your anxiety.

There are many types of informal mindfulness practices, including meditation and activity-based exercises, as well as formal mindfulness courses and psychotherapies, such as mindfulness-based stress reduction (Kabat-Zinn 2009) and mindfulness-based cognitive therapy (Segal, Williams, and Teasdale 2002). Engaging in mindfulness practices will foster your ability to mindfully respond to the experiences in your life, which will lead to improved overall mental health. In the remainder of this chapter, we will present several informal ways of attending to your present-moment experiences with less judgment and less reactivity. By so doing, you will be well on your way to outsmarting anxiety!

Outsmarting Anxiety Skill #1:
Pay attention to your anxiety.

Suggested Practices

Before going into the first exercises, we would like to give you some general guidelines for mindfulness practice.

Set aside five to twenty minutes each day for a full week for the purpose of applying these simple mindfulness exercises to your daily life. Choose a time that works well with your schedule and when you are not likely to be interrupted. If you can, choose a time that will work well for you every day of the week, such as soon after you wake up or after you come home from work.

Try to be consistent with your practice. Life will invariably present you with many obstacles, big and small, but try not to let these get in the way of your practice. Remember, the benefit of practicing mindfulness is to learn to attend to your life experiences in a nonjudgmental and nonreactive way. We encourage you to practice mindfulness no matter what's going on in your life. Do you have a cold? Practice mindfulness. Are you stressed at work? Practice mindfulness. Did you just win the lottery? Practice mindfulness. Regardless of any excuse you have—good or bad—practice mindfulness!

Develop strategies for reminding yourself to practice each day, such as writing the time on your calendar. Practice only for the amount of time you choose (you can use a kitchen or smartphone timer to help you practice for the same amount of time each day), and practice in a quiet and comfortable setting.

Try not to judge yourself or your abilities. Judging your mindfulness practice is antithetical to the very idea of mindfulness. Training yourself to be mindful is similar to training a puppy to walk on a leash. At first, the puppy will probably pull away from you, lag behind, run around you, or do just about anything except walk down the sidewalk. To teach a puppy to properly walk on a leash, world-class trainers recommend that you calmly and gently guide the puppy along the path. So imagine that mindfulness is the path and your brain is the puppy. Be calm, gentle, and kind to yourself. While practicing mindfulness, especially while you are learning more fundamental concepts, remember that it's normal for you to get distracted, for your mind to wander, or for you to occasionally forget your goal. When this happens, try to simply start over without judging yourself.

All of the mindfulness practices in this book are for beginners and experienced meditators alike. Although some of the exercises may seem simple, it can take months or years for people to cultivate a mindful stance toward life, and even then, no one is absolutely perfect at it all the time. Also, try not to judge these exercises as easy or difficult—allow them to simply be something you experience, whether for five seconds or five full minutes.

Visit http://www.newharbinger.com/34169 for audio recordings of several of the mindfulness practices. You may download these for your personal use. On the website, you will also find worksheets to help you process your experiences during the mindfulness exercises. These include questions for reflection, considerations for enhancing your practices, and instructions for extending the time of your mindfulness practice.

Exercise 2.1: **Conscious Observation**   Find a quiet and comfortable place where you can sit upright on a chair (with an unsupported back) or on a cushion on the floor. Adopt a relaxed but alert posture. Once you are seated, set a timer to alert you when sixty seconds have passed. For one minute, with your eyes open and while breathing normally, observe each breath you take. Attuning yourself to the process of breathing—inhaling and exhaling—is your only goal. This exercise might sound incredibly straightforward, but one minute can seem like an eternity, especially if you are distracted by bodily sensations, aspects of your environment (such as the ticking of a clock or noise outside of your room or house), or even your own thoughts or emotions. If this happens, simply bring your attention back to the exercise and remember the goal: to fully observe your breathing for one minute. Do this a few times a day, with the idea that it's not a personal contest or challenge—it's simply an observational experience without judgment or reactivity.

Exercise 2.2: **Nonreactive Stance**   Find a quiet and comfortable place where you can sit upright on a chair (with an unsupported back) or on a cushion on the floor. Adopt a relaxed but alert posture. Once you are seated, set a timer to alert you when three minutes have passed. For those three minutes, try to practice mindfully focusing on a simple mental image of your choosing. For example, you may choose to focus on a blue circle, an orange square, or a purple rectangle. These are only suggestions; choose any *simple* object that comes to mind. For three minutes, try to visualize the object as clearly as possible. Notice its shape, its edges, its dimensions, the vibrancy of the color, and its overall size. Simply try to see the image as clearly as possible. If you lose your concentration or if your mind is flooded with emotions or thoughts, try not to judge yourself or those emotions or thoughts; simply reengage with the exercise. Try your best not to react to external stimuli or even other ideas, thoughts, or images that enter your mind. Your goal is simply to focus on the image of your choice for three minutes. Do this once every day for the entire week.

Exercise 2.3: **Nonjudgmental Stance**   Find a quiet and comfortable place where you can sit upright on a chair (with an unsupported back) or on a cushion on the floor. Adopt a relaxed but alert posture. Once you are seated, set a timer to alert you when five minutes have passed. Choose any mundane object in your house or office and hold it in your hand. Try not to put too much thought into the object you choose. For five minutes, hold the object in your hand and allow it to absorb your attention. Simply observe the object without evaluating it or applying emotion to it. Allow yourself to fully appreciate the object's properties—its dimensions, weight, temperature, texture, and so on. Try to observe the object with as much clarity as possible. If you lose your concentration or if your mind is flooded with emotions or thoughts, try not to judge yourself or those emotions or thoughts; simply reengage with the exercise. Try your best not to react to external stimuli or even other ideas, thoughts, or images that enter your mind. Your goal is simply to focus on the object of your choice for five minutes. Do this at least three times during the week.

Exercise 2.4: **Combined Nonreactive and Nonjudgmental Stance**   For this exercise, you will need some type of edible seed or nut (such as a pumpkin or soy seed, a walnut, or a pistachio) or a piece of dried fruit (especially if you are allergic to nuts). Find a quiet and comfortable place where you can sit upright on a chair (with an unsupported back) or on a cushion on the floor. Adopt a relaxed but alert posture. Once you are seated, set a timer to alert you when five minutes have passed. For the next five minutes, your goal is to fully absorb the sensory properties of the food you have chosen.

Start by holding it and examining it in detail, almost as if you had never seen this type of food before. Examine its features, colors, shading, and texture. Also notice its weight, how it fits in your hand, and how it feels when you touch it with your fingers. Then, hold it up to your nose and smell it. Notice its aroma or any subtle fragrance it has. Next, place it on your tongue. When you are ready, begin to taste it with your tongue and eventually chew it. Notice where in your mouth you chew it, how long it takes you to chew, and what flavors emanate from it. Before swallowing the food, notice how its texture and taste have changed from when it was in its original form. Again, when you feel ready to swallow the food, see whether you can first detect the urge to swallow so that you are consciously and purposely attending to your own urges. Once you swallow the food, notice the taste or any flavors that remain in your mouth.

Throughout this mindfulness experience, practice not reacting to or judging the various sensory properties of the food. If judgments or reactions do occur, simply notice them and refocus on your goal to experience the food. Repeat this practice a few times throughout the week, and try it with different foods.

Exercise 2.5: **Combined Nonreactive and Nonjudgmental Stance with Interoceptive Awareness**   This mindfulness practice is different from the others in that it's not scheduled or planned. The purpose of this exercise is to teach you to take a break from your routine and be more purposeful in the present moment. At any time of day, even if you are busy or your life feels hectic, follow these steps:

1. Stop whatever you are doing and ask yourself, *What is my experience right now?* Adopting a nonjudgmental stance (accepting your present state rather than avoiding or suppressing any experiences, including those that are unpleasant) and without reacting (without trying to change

certain thoughts, emotions, bodily sensations, and so on), take about a minute to notice any bodily sensations, emotions, or thoughts you are having.

2. Focus your full attention on the movements and sensations associated with your breathing, noticing each time you breathe in and out. Do this for about one minute.

3. Allow your awareness of your breath to grow into awareness of your entire body. Notice your special orientation, your posture, and any sensations that are present. Again, do this for about one minute, without judgment or reactivity.

Do this at least twice during the week and preferably in different settings (for example, at home and at work).

◌◌◌

By practicing these mindfulness exercises, you will hone your ability to notice your emotions in a nonreactive manner. Mindfully approaching your emotions can be similar to mindfully approaching your food, as in practice 2.4. This nonreactive and nonjudgmental approach enables you to foster crucial distance from your emotions, as if you are experiencing them with a sense of novelty and childlike curiosity. By directing your attention to present-moment experiences, you can appreciate all the complex facets of your emotional experience without being weighed down by turmoil or feeling a need to control your negative thoughts. It will be important that you continue to develop and practice these skills in concert with the other techniques we will present in later chapters. Remember, persistence and patience while practicing mindfulness will promote inner peace and tranquility.

Don't Let Anxiety Run Your Life

chapter 3

Confronting Your Anxiety

Imagine sitting at the top of a roller coaster, high above the ground, about to go into a 100-mile-per-hour dive. Or imagine you're in a steel cage, about to be lowered into the ocean to swim with great white sharks. In either of these situations, you might notice a sense of nervousness—manifested by sweaty palms, a thud-like pulsing of your heart throughout your body, jitteriness, a sinking feeling in your stomach, and racing thoughts. How would you react? Would you panic, or would you try to override your anxiety to experience the thrill of a lifetime?

In everyday life, people face many less extreme adventures, yet they still may feel as if they are in a cage surrounded by sharks. For some people, something as simple as talking on the phone, noticing their own fast heartbeat, or having to touch a germ-ridden bathroom door handle can lead to excessive anxiety.

When anxiety strikes, do you fight it or do you walk away? How does your anxiety affect your behavior? In this chapter, we will teach you how to manage your anxiety by gradually confronting your fears using a research-based intervention known as *exposure*. We will do this by first exploring how avoidance behaviors can sometimes exacerbate your anxiety. We will then review how early learning experiences contribute to anxiety and how to mindfully and effectively manage your behavior to reduce your anxiety in stressful moments.

The Vicious Cycle of Anxiety and Avoidance

Avoidance is a hallmark of anxiety. When you actively avoid the things that make you fearful or anxious, you also avoid the emotional experiences associated with anxiety. In the short term, this can seem like a sensible approach; after all, most people don't want to purposefully experience anxiety. Nonetheless, this strategy can be quite problematic because it denies you the opportunity to confront your fears. Not only does this maintain your problematic relationship with the feared object or situation, it strengthens your anxiety response for future encounters. This cycle leads to increased anxiety and worry, loss of confidence in your ability to cope, more physical symptoms of anxiety, and increased use of safety behaviors.

For example, if you are scared of dogs and you do your best to avoid them, you still might encounter one; however, the more you avoid dogs, the more your anxiety grows. Your avoidance essentially feeds the cycle of anxiety by preserving your fear and perpetuating a maladaptive approach to managing your anxiety through avoidance. If you want to stop this cycle, you will need to confront your anxiety by purposefully and gradually subjecting yourself to the things that make you anxious.

What Is Avoidance?

One surprisingly simple way to overcome your anxiety is to consider your characteristic ways of behaving when you are anxious. Your behavior is incredibly strongly linked to your emotions, thoughts, and bodily sensations, all of which are highly activated during times of anxiety. In fact, behavioral responses to fear and anxiety rarely, if ever, originate from an actual object or situation; instead, they arise because of the problematic relationship you have to your fears. The ways you choose to behave during times of anxiety both contribute to and reinforce this maladaptive relationship over time. Thus, one crucial way of changing how you feel during moments of anxiety is to behave differently than you have in the past by purposefully and gradually subjecting yourself to the things that make you anxious and that you normally try to avoid. Later in this chapter, we will teach you some techniques for doing just that.

As mentioned in the introduction, anxiety, as well as the way you behave in response to your anxiety, is a highly subjective experience that varies from person to person. Even your own anxiety symptoms and their intensity vary depending on the situation and its context. If you want to test either of these notions, think about the various reactions people might have if someone let loose a mouse in a crowded lecture hall. Some people might freeze or scream, others might jump onto their chair for safety, and yet others might have only some mild or fleeting anxiety symptoms and then watch the panicked crowd with amusement. These various reactions are based on the ways in which people relate to the prospect of coming into contact with the mouse.

Let's say you're taking a class that meets for a lecture every day. In terms of your own anxiety, think about how you might react to someone releasing a mouse in the lecture hall one Monday. Now imagine that someone releases a mouse in the lecture hall on Tuesday as well. And Wednesday. How might your reaction change after someone releases a mouse every day for a week? And then a month? Even if you detest mice, we guarantee that after a full week, let alone a month, your anxiety in the presence of that mouse (and other mice) will diminish, due to the effect of repeated exposure to the mouse.

Practice Consider how your anxious reactions might change from time to time and what modifies them. For example, you might be more or less anxious about something depending on your environment (such as whether you are at home or out in public), the time of day, whom you are with (family, friends, strangers, and so on), how you are feeling (tired? happy? sick? content?), or even how often the experience has occurred and for how long.

What Is Anxious Avoidance?

Despite normal variations in how individuals experience anxiety, some symptoms, especially in terms of behavior, are widely shared. Behavioral symptoms of anxiety refer to how you act in an effort to cope or remove yourself from a perceived threat and unpleasant experience of anxiety. One of the most common behavioral tendencies is *anxious avoidance*, a normal inclination to protect yourself by exerting *some* level of control over supposed threatening aspects of your environment. If you have ever refused to cross a tall bridge, get a shot at the doctor's office, or give a speech in front of your peers because you imagined it would be unpleasant, that's anxious avoidance! It's an intuitive and self-reinforcing behavioral tendency that most people exhibit at some point in their lives; for others, it's chronic.

In the short term, avoiding unpleasant experiences makes you feel less anxious because you were able to avoid situations you feared. It can be a helpful and adaptive process! Nevertheless, it's not possible (or appropriate) to avoid all the unpleasant experiences in life. Indeed, the more you avoid, the more your anxiety builds up in the presence of whatever it is you have been avoiding. When used excessively or inappropriately, avoidance thus becomes problematic.

Anxious avoidance manifests in many ways and to varying degrees. Following are some common avoidance strategies:

- Intentional avoidance (for example, driving on back roads instead of the highway or refusing to attend parties or other social engagements out of fear of being judged or evaluated)

- Escaping from anxiety-producing situations (for example, leaving a crowded store or market to avoid feeling panicked)

- Using safety behaviors (for example, carrying calming medications with you or insisting that a friend or family member accompany you throughout the day)

- Using distractions (for example, listening to music while having a tooth drilled, or instructing a child to look at a cartoon on the wall while he or she receives an immunization)

- Engaging in maladaptive coping behaviors (such as excessive alcohol or drug use)

Anxious avoidance can also be characterized by the degree to which you avoid anxiety-producing situations. In many situations, it's possible to fully *or* partially avoid anxiety-producing situations (for example, refusing to fly altogether versus flying only under the influence of calming medications).

Practice   Take a moment to assess the level and type of avoidance you tend to employ in those situations in your life when you feel most anxious. It may be helpful to write down situations or objects in your life that make you feel anxious (such as "meeting new people" or "door handles or knobs"). Then, take time to rate each one according to how often you use avoidance (such as "85 percent of the time" or "as often as possible") and what kind of avoidance you use (for example, "intentional avoidance; I stay at home as often as possible and avoid talking to colleagues at work.").

Why Do You Avoid?

In a recent study, researchers asked participants to think of a specific time in their life when they felt happy and then to specify an amount of money they would be willing to pay to re-create that experience. Participants were then asked to place a monetary value on re-creating other emotional experiences ranging from positive (such as joy and calm) to negative (such as regret and fear). Not surprisingly, people were, on average, willing to pay more money to experience positive emotions than they were to avoid negative emotions. The researchers then repeated their study with more participants to confirm their findings. In the second study, results generally stayed the same, but there was one noticeable difference: people were willing to pay *more* money to avoid fearful experiences than they were to re-create feelings of excitement, calm and tranquility, or self-pride (Lau, White, and Schnall 2013). This study tells us that people are fairly well motivated to avoid feelings associated with anxiety and fear, even at the expense of experiencing more positive emotions.

In our own work in treating anxiety, we routinely encounter people who choose avoidance-based responses despite knowing it unfavorably affects their psychological well-being and in spite of more rational ways of coping. To understand *why* this happens, we have to turn to psychological theories on early learning experiences, including conditioning. In psychology, we define *learning* as a long-term change in behavior based on an experience. There are generally two types of learning; both are forms of *conditioning* (learning by association), termed *classical* and *operant* conditioning.

The Impact of Early Learning Experiences on Anxiety

Almost all children develop a fear of the dark (also known as nyctophobia) during their toddler years. It's an interesting phenomenon because during infancy, most babies contentedly sleep in their cribs in dark rooms, yet around age three, darkness suddenly becomes cause for concern. Toddlers tend to overestimate the probability of danger in a dark bedroom because they have enough imagination to believe monsters *could be* lurking in the shadows, but they don't yet have enough cognitive ability to distinguish fantasy from reality. Initially when the fear is present, children attempt to outright avoid the dark by demanding the use of nightlights or will tolerate the dark only if a parent is present while they fall asleep. Over time, children's fear of the dark typically wanes, partly thanks to normal development and maturation but also because they *learn* that the shadows in their bedroom don't actually harbor monsters. This learning takes place as they gradually and purposefully confront their anxiety (by sleeping in the dark, despite their fears). They essentially have to change their relationship with the dark through experience. However, if they don't learn to change their relationship, they will miss opportunities to appropriately confront their anxiety.

Conditioning

If you have ever taken a psychology course or read an introductory psychology text, you likely came across the work of Ivan Pavlov, a Russian physiologist who trained dogs to salivate at the sound of a tuning fork. Pavlov achieved this result through *stimulus pairing*—in this case, pairing the sound of a tuning fork with the presentation of food. Pavlov's dogs, like most dogs, naturally salivated at the sight of food; over time, they came to associate the sight of food with the sound of the tuning fork, so that eventually the sound of the tuning fork alone was enough to cause them to salivate in anticipation of being fed.

Dogs automatically salivate in the presence of food—they don't choose to salivate or even think about whether to salivate. It just happens. Because this behavior is involuntary, Pavlov was able to change what triggered it by changing the dogs' experience. All he had to do was give them a reason to salivate when they heard a tuning fork (or, potentially, were exposed to any stimulus of his choosing). They then came to equate that particular sound with food.

One of the most important things to remember about the type of learning that Pavlov's work illustrates, known as *classical conditioning*, is that the learning takes place automatically and without the learner's conscious awareness. Classical conditioning is useful in everyday life, both for animals and for people. If you have ever owned a pet, you have no doubt witnessed classical conditioning in action. Cats, for example, often show up to the kitchen whenever you use a can opener, regardless of whether you are opening a can of cat food or something for yourself. Farmers have used classical conditioning to protect their sheep from predation by foxes by sprinkling a powder on sheep meat that temporarily causes digestive problems for foxes. Over time, the foxes learn to avoid killing sheep to avoid stomachaches. In people, the effects of classical conditioning can be found almost everywhere. Have you ever felt hungry after a TV commercial break? Chances are you had just seen a commercial for some type of food. Have you ever been moved to tears by an older song? If so, it was probably because you associated the song with a sad or happy memory. Have you ever started gagging at the smell of something, perhaps Limburger cheese (often described as smelling like human feet)? Past associations with foul-smelling stimuli can sometimes instantly make us gag or even throw up. (If you want to see an example of classical conditioning in action, the TV show *The Office* demonstrates this phenomenon with two of its main characters in episode 15 of season 3. Essentially, one of the characters plays a prank on his colleague by training him to salivate for a mint upon hearing the chime from a computer).

Practice   Think of some automatic reactions or reflexive responses you have to your daily environment, including objects and situations that make you feel anxious. For example, how do you react when you hear music playing from an ice cream truck? Or how do you feel when you experience the smell of a doctor's office or a hospital?

Fear conditioning, a type of classical conditioning, is a behavioral principle of how people learn to predict aversive events. Fear conditioning helps explain why some people are anxious and why they might have a difficult time confronting their anxiety. If, as a young child, you happened to be stung by a bee, you likely developed a healthy fear of bees and other insects that looked like bees (wasps, hornets, yellow jackets, and so on). Perhaps you never were stung but nevertheless have a fear of bees, either after hearing about them from a parent or friend or seeing someone get stung.

Fear, as it turns out, is a fairly universal phenomenon. It's made even more salient because of how our bodies respond physically, including increases in both heart and respiration rate and release of stress-related hormones. Along with these symptoms, fear becomes even more significant to humans because of our unique cognitive abilities to develop a relationship with fear through our thoughts, emotions, and memories.

The second type of learning, *operant conditioning*, involves voluntary behavior (as opposed to automatic or reflexive behavior, as in classical conditioning). Operant conditioning received its name because individuals operate (behave) based on influences from their environment, including both positive and negative consequences. This form of learning is a useful way of training animals or people to behave in a certain way. Dogs will do almost anything for a tasty treat and can easily be trained to behave in complex ways (believe it or not, dogs have been trained using operant conditioning to drive cars!). Humans are also easily trained to behave in specific ways. There are many examples of operant conditioning in your everyday life: you go to work to get paid, you wear your seatbelt to avoid a fine, you study for a test if you want to pass it, you do good work at school or your job to avoid being criticized, or you take a dollar from your child's allowance if he or she says a bad word or neglects a chore. Do you notice a common theme among these examples? Essentially, operant conditioning can be used to shape behavior, and even control it, based on positive and negative actions. It also can help you respond differently to your anxiety, especially when used during the exposure practices later in this chapter.

Practice   Think of some operant conditioning responses you have to your daily environment. For example, have you ever behaved in a certain way to obtain a reward or avoid punishment? Try to think of examples from multiple contexts in your life, such as at home, at work, at school, and during social interactions.

Shaping Your Anxiety Responses Through Reinforcement

The tools used to shape behavior in operant conditioning are known as *positive and negative reinforcement* and *positive and negative punishment*. Reinforcement is used to *increase* a desirable behavior, whereas punishment is used to *decrease* an undesirable behavior. A good deal of your operant behavior is based on external influences (such as other people or the conditions of your environment) of reinforcement and punishment. The positive and negative aspects of reinforcement and punishment refer to applying and withholding (or removing) a stimulus, respectively, to increase (encourage) or decrease (discourage) behavior. Some people find these distinctions slightly confusing, especially because the terms "positive" and "negative" and "reinforcement" and "punishment" are being used in different ways than is customary, but don't despair—refer to figure 3.1 for a couple of real-life examples of each.

Figure 3.1. Positive and Negative Reinforcement and Punishment

		Positive (Apply)	Negative (Withhold)
Reinforcement (Increase Behavior)		**Positive Reinforcement** *Apply something to increase behavior.*	**Negative Reinforcement** *Withhold something to increase behavior.*
Punishment (Decrease Behavior)		**Positive Punishment** *Apply something to decrease behavior.*	**Negative Punishment** *Withhold something to decrease behavior.*

Positive Reinforcement (apply something to increase a behavior):

a. Jake's health insurance company gives him a discount on his monthly premium if he walks at least 2 miles per day at least five times a week.

   A discount is being applied to increase a healthy behavior.

b. Mae has social anxiety, but she rewards herself for talking to at least two people who are new to her at an office gathering.

A reward is being applied for increasing prosocial behavior.

Negative Reinforcement (withhold or remove something to increase a behavior):

a. When Arissa, a five-year-old girl, screams and cries fearfully while waiting in line to see Santa Claus, her parents take her home.

The parents remove the anxiety of seeing Santa, thereby increasing positive behavior in the moment, but inadvertently increasing the likelihood that Arissa will scream and cry again the next time she is unhappy.

b. When Malik, who is worried about his health, calls his doctor's office, the staff reassure him about his symptoms.

The staff's reassurance assuages Malik's worries, thereby increasing the likelihood that he will call the next time he is worried about his health.

Positive Punishment (apply something to decrease a behavior):

a. Claire's mobile phone rings in the middle of a work meeting, and her boss reprimands her for not turning off her phone.

The boss's reprimand was applied to decrease the behavior of bringing a phone to meetings.

b. Every time Andrew obsesses about being con-
taminated by germs after using a public rest-
room, he snaps a rubber band on his wrist to
remind him to stop obsessing.

*The mild pain of snapping the rubber band is
meant to decrease the obsessions.*

Negative Punishment (withhold or remove something
to decrease a behavior):

a. Connor is hurriedly driving home from work
when he is stopped by a police officer and given a
$500 ticket for speeding.

*Connor's money is being taken away to decrease
the frequency of future speeding behavior.*

b. Nia loves going to the symphony, but while there,
she has a panic attack and abruptly leaves before
the concert is finished.

*Leaving the symphony decreases panic symp-
toms. (Note: It might be easy to confuse this example
with the principles of reinforcement—thinking that
leaving the concert will increase the likelihood that
Nia will have panic attacks at future concerts—but
in this case, Nia wants to **decrease** her panic symptoms, so she removes something she typically enjoys.)*

Although learning about conditioning and reinforcement may feel like an academic exercise, these important
concepts will help you better manage your anxiety.
Specifically, both reinforcement and punishment can help
you identify and alter the ways you behave so that you can
stop the vicious cycle of anxiety and appropriately confront
your anxiety.

First, positive reinforcement can help you gradually confront your fears. This entails using rewards, or aspects of your environment that motivate you to respond by appropriately approaching what you are afraid of, and strengthening the use of *approach responses* in future situations (instead of continuing to use avoidance responses). For example, if you have a fear of germs and your goal is to be able to touch door handles without becoming too anxious, you might add money to a jar each time you touch a door handle, which you can then spend any way you like. The money becomes a motivation for you to touch door handles (which is an approach response). (Note: When using a "motivation jar," choose the amount of money you will add beforehand, ensuring that it's proportionate to the behavior. For example, decide that you will give yourself a dollar for every door handle you touch. A penny would not be motivating enough, and fifty dollars would be motivating for the wrong reasons.)

Second, in anxiety, avoidance is fundamentally a form of negative reinforcement. Each time you avoid that which makes you fearful or anxious, you are rewarding yourself, because your behavior removes the unwanted stimulus or feeling. Thus, the more you avoid anxiety-provoking situations, the more likely you are to keep avoiding them. This pattern interferes with your goals, essentially because it helps you avoid the experience of fear and anxiety that's a normal part of meeting challenges.

Physiological Influences on Behavior in Anxiety

Emotions have long been of interest to scientists and theorists, especially in terms of their relationship to physiological processes, or the physical symptoms that accompany an emotion. Try, if you will, to think about a time when you experienced a moderately intense emotion. Perhaps you were driving on the highway and another car suddenly pulled in front of you, nearly causing an accident. Or think of a time when you had to stand up for yourself and confront someone. What emotions did you experience? Conceivably, you might have experienced some level of anger, impatience, frustration, or maybe even rage. Now, consider the physical symptoms you experienced or how your body reacted. Was your heart pounding? Did you feel shaky? Was your mouth dry? Did you feel flushed? Did you sweat more than normal or suffer an intense feeling of dread? If so, or if you experienced similar physical symptoms, you were experiencing the physical aspect of an emotion.

Leading theories on emotion all highlight the important relationship between emotions and physiological arousal in anxiety and how these interact with early learning (conditioning) experiences to influence your behavior under threatening conditions. The physical symptoms that you experience when you feel anxious or fearful are influenced not only by your immediate environment but also by your perceived ability to cope with a specific threat. You likely use one of two types of coping when you feel anxious: *active* or *passive* coping. You are more likely to use active coping strategies—that is, to fight or flee—when you believe you can overcome or escape from a threat. These strategies can be either adaptive or maladaptive depending on the context of your fear or anxiety, but a general rule of thumb is that confronting your anxiety is usually adaptive whereas fleeing from your anxiety is maladaptive. For example, if you are at a summer barbecue with your friends and you suddenly have a panic attack, confronting your anxious thoughts, emotions, and physiological feelings is inherently more adaptive than fleeing from your discomfort to a place of "safety." You are more likely to use passive coping—that is, to freeze—when escape from a threat seems impossible. For example, if a bee is chasing you in your backyard, you might be inclined to confront it by swatting at it, or perhaps you're able to run inside your house and close the door before the bee stings you. But if escape from the threat of the bee seems impossible, such as if it were to land on your arm, you might freeze in the hope it won't sting you. In general, using more active-oriented coping approaches paired with positive reinforcements is a useful way to manage your anxiety. Active and adaptive coping is what helps you confront and work through your fears rather than remaining anxious, stressed, or even depressed (LeDoux and Gorman 2001).

Overcoming Avoidance

By now, it should be no surprise that to modify your anxiety, you have to modify your behavior and confront your anxiety. But you might be wondering *how* to do this, especially if your anxious avoidance is a deeply ingrained and habitual response to your anxiety. To that end, you need a deeper understanding of *when and why* avoidance is problematic.

First of all, avoidance of anxiety-producing stimuli enhances your sense of a loss of control, which in turn diminishes your brain's ability to think logically and rationally (Arnsten 2009). In practical terms, this means that you tend to rely on automatic instincts when faced with a perceived threat to your survival. In many cases, your nervous system reinforces your tendency to avoid; after all, who wants to experience queasiness, sweaty palms, and a dry mouth when you can much more easily avoid the scary aspects of life?

Second, anxious avoidance inhibits learning (LeDoux 2015). If you fear coming into contact with a deadly germ, washing your hands every time you touch an unhygienic surface will help thwart your anxiety response; however, this solves your problem only in the very short term and creates greater problems for the future. That's because each time you avoid touching an unhygienic surface, you lose yet another opportunity to reduce your fear of germs through learning that you can touch the unhygienic surface and not get sick.

Third, avoidance enhances dysfunctional beliefs related to your anxiety. More simply, when you avoid confronting your anxiety, you remove the opportunity to test your thoughts and to challenge the pathological relationship you have to the threatening situation. Imagine a friend who has social anxiety and avoids social interaction at all costs. He confides to you that he wants to make friends or develop a romantic relationship but believes himself to be "awkward, unworthy of affection, and pathetic." Every time your friend engages in anxious avoidance behaviors, whether they include avoiding interactions at all costs, drinking excessively before parties, or looking at his phone as a distraction at parties, he loses the important opportunity to test the truth of his negative thoughts about himself.

Fourth and finally, anxious avoidance reinforces the chronicity of your anxiety, meaning it may get worse over time, it may include new fears, or your responses to it may become increasingly and overtly avoidant.

Optimizing Your Anxiety

A well-known principle in psychology, especially to those of us who treat and research anxiety, is the Yerkes-Dodson law (Yerkes and Dodson 1908). It's a simple, yet important, concept with regard to how you manage your anxiety. Recall from the introduction to this book that anxiety is generally thought to be a helpful and adaptive process. For example, if you want to obtain a high grade on a test, physiological and mental arousal will motivate you to study the subject material; however, if you have too little or too much arousal, your performance on the test will be adversely affected and likely decrease. Take a moment to review the graph of this relationship shown in figure 3.2.

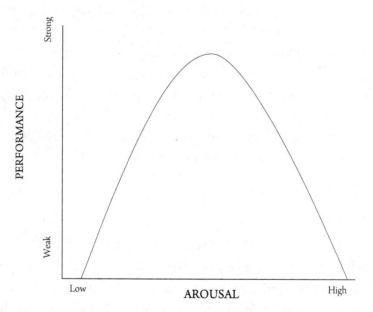

Figure 3.2. The Yerkes-Dodson Law

Research on the Yerkes-Dodson law has found that different tasks require different levels of arousal for optimal performance. For example, you might need more physiological and mental arousal to perform well in front of hundreds at a concert recital, but less physiological and mental arousal to successfully give a speech to a small group of supportive coworkers. On the other hand, you might need a lower level of physiological and mental arousal to complete an intellectually demanding task (lower levels facilitate concentration) versus a higher level of arousal for tasks involving stamina or persistence (higher levels increase motivation).

Practice   Take a moment to assess your optimal levels of physiological and mental arousal for those times when you feel performance pressure. Now compare the ideal level to what's true for you. For example, if you have social anxiety, what would be an optimal level of physiological and mental arousal for you to give a speech to ten people? To do this, plot on the graph how your performance (vertical axis) and your arousal (horizontal axis) intersect. If it's helpful, think of your performance as a range on a continuum from weak to strong and your arousal as a range on a continuum from low to medium to high. How would you characterize your current state of physiological and mental arousal? Is it balanced, or is it skewed to one end of the graph or the other?

Exposure

One of the most effective and important ways to deal with your anxiety and fears, whether they are rational or not, is to gently confront them. As the title of this chapter suggests, running from your anxiety isn't helpful and likely does more harm than good over time. To stop running, we encourage you to gradually confront your anxiety and fear through the use of *exposure*, or purposefully subjecting yourself to your fears. Exposure, in many ways, is the exact opposite of anxious avoidance. Exposure works by slowly reducing fears associated with a threatening stimulus and also decreases your anxiety and distress. Over time and with enough practice, exposure can help improve your relationship to a feared object or situation through *mastery* of the experience, in which you deliberately develop a sense of ease and control over your fear, which leads to increased confidence in your ability to regulate your emotions.

The three main goals of exposure are:

1. To teach you to accept uncertainty and lack of control about the feared object or situation.

2. To teach you to activate problematic emotions and thoughts so that you may challenge them upon confronting the feared object or situation.

3. To teach you to habituate yourself to your physiological responses to, emotional reactions to, and unhelpful beliefs about the feared object or situation.

Exposure can be beneficial for many types of anxiety: simple phobias, obsessive-compulsive disorder, social anxiety disorder, generalized anxiety disorder, panic disorder, agoraphobia, post-traumatic stress disorder, and more. Although exposure primarily entails behaviorally confronting your anxiety, it also includes confronting related thoughts, emotions, and bodily sensations through a hierarchy of events designed to build your tolerance.

To illustrate, imagine that you have a fear of heights, also known as acrophobia. You first would want to identify the specific behavior you hope to modify (your *behavioral target*). For this example, let's assume that you want to go on vacation with your family, but the driving route entails crossing a rather tall bridge. Thus, exposure might include first looking at pictures of the bridge from various angles, watching videos of people driving across the bridge, thinking about crossing the bridge, driving over smaller bridges with a progressive escalation in size, driving to the bridge to see it in person, and eventually driving over the bridge. (This is a somewhat simplified example.)

There are several types of exposures, all of which vary in their approach and difficulty with regard to implementing them in your own life. These include:

- **In vivo exposure:** Directly facing a feared object, situation, or activity in real life

   For example, someone with a fear of snakes might first look at pictures of snakes, with the goal of working up to handling actual snakes under supervision.

- **Imaginal exposure:** Vividly imagining a feared object or situation

   For example, someone with a fear of germs might be asked to imagine coming into contact with germs and how he or she might react in terms of emotions, bodily sensations, behaviors, or even thoughts.

- **Virtual reality exposure:** Virtual reality technology can be used when in vivo exposure is not realistic.

   For example, someone with a fear of flying might use a virtual reality flight simulator to experience the sights, sounds, and even smells of riding in an airplane. Many of these virtual reality exposures are conducted in psychologists' offices.

- **Interoceptive exposure:** Deliberately bringing on physical sensations that are harmless, yet feared.

  For example, someone who is prone to panicking might be instructed to run up and down stairs to create a sense of breathlessness or an increased heart rate; spin around in a chair to induce dizziness; or breathe through a straw to bring on feelings of hyperventilation. The idea is for the person to learn that these sensations aren't dangerous and don't necessarily indicate that anything is wrong.

The idea behind exposure is that you confront your fears through new conditioning experiences. Each step in an exposure hierarchy may lead to anxiety, but as Yerkes and Dodson taught us, you need some anxiety to perform optimally while confronting your fear. We fully expect you to feel anxious during each exposure, perhaps more than you would expect or like; however, we know that through multiple exposures, your anxiety will eventually decrease so you can master the current step of your exposure hierarchy. Using the example above, in which you are afraid to cross a bridge, perhaps you would experience more anxiety, especially in the form of increased physiological arousal, while watching videos of the bridge than you would while simply looking at pictures. In that case, we would encourage you to spend more time with that particular step of the exposure until your anxiety is significantly reduced. We also don't

want you to take an all-or-nothing approach to exposure—
that is, to face your fear all at once or not at all. If you take on
too much anxiety in a single step, you may panic and back
out of the exposure, which would leave you even more afraid
to attempt it in future. The best exposures entail a delicate
balance between confronting and avoiding.

Integrating Mindfulness and Exposure

Mindfulness can greatly enhance your ability to confront your anxiety and reduce anxious avoidance. Notably,
mindfulness can increase your attentional capacity, which
facilitates greater awareness of your behavioral avoidance
tendencies. Primarily, mindfulness will enable you to be
more aware of your moment-to-moment activities so that
you can more closely examine your anxiety and its impact
on your behavior and general functioning. It may also facilitate *decentering*, or the ability to perceive your thoughts and
feelings as temporary and transient rather than permanent.
In this way, mindfulness allows you to change your relationship to your anxiety by broadening your perspective and
learning to accept and confront your experiences rather
than running away from them. Mindfulness may also
enhance learning, especially from exposures, by helping you
more accurately describe and label your feelings, which will
give you greater insight into the relationships among your
thoughts, emotions, bodily sensations, and behaviors.
Finally, mindfulness may change the way you think about
anxiety-provoking experiences. Without mindfulness, you
may be prone to think negatively about your experience at a
party, for example, and label yourself as socially inept;
however, by taking a more mindful stance, you may be able

to interrupt these thought processes and learn to think more accurately about your experience (Treanor 2011).

Outsmarting Anxiety Skill #2:
Confront, rather than avoid, your anxiety.

Suggested Practices

First, here are some tips for confronting your anxiety, to guide you as you practice exposing yourself to objects and situations that you fear:

- Set an achievable goal that identifies a fear you wish to overcome (for example, "I want to target my fear of heights by riding over a tall bridge").

- Develop an exposure plan (listing all the aspects of your goal, from least to most frightening) with graduated steps, to help you slowly confront your anxiety.

- Remember, exposures can include both imaginal (thinking about a feared object or situation in your head) and in vivo components.

- Rate your level of distress and anxiety (for example, on a scale from 0 to 10, with 0 representing no distress and 10 representing significant distress) before, during, and after each step of the exposure plan.

- Eliminate safety nets, or ways of coping that make your anxiety easier to manage (such as using substances, people, or various distractions).

- Repeat each step of the exposure as often as needed or until you notice a significant decline in your anxiety. Use the distress scale as a guide!

- After completing an exposure in full, keep repeating the exposure in the future, which will help with long-term anxiety maintenance. This will be more beneficial than practicing exposure for short-term or moment-to-moment emotion management.

- Summarize one or two main learning experiences from each exposure that you can apply to similar situations in the future.

- Remember to prioritize your own physical and mental safety by choosing exposures that are appropriate to your ability and capacity. Remember the Yerkes–Dodson Law: too much exposure or too little exposure will not be as helpful as an exposure that creates only some anxiety and discomfort.

Exercise 3.1: **Confront Your Anxiety in Your Imagination** For this mindfulness practice, find a quiet and comfortable place where you can sit upright on a chair (with an unsupported back) or on a cushion on the floor. Adopt a relaxed but alert posture. Once you are seated, set a timer to alert you when five minutes have passed.

1. Identify something that you more than routinely avoid due to anxiety, and specify a behavioral target for exposure. For example, some people avoid managing their monthly bills because thinking about finances makes them extremely

anxious. Perhaps you avoid thoughts, feelings, and behaviors associated with a past traumatic experience.

2. Think about what you do to avoid feeling anxious and how you would like to confront your avoidance behavior, including imagining yourself confronting the object or situation that you fear with acceptance rather than reactivity or avoidance. Using the two examples above, you might avoid managing monthly bills through procrastination activities (surfing the Internet, watching TV, and so on), or you might avoid remembering a car accident by refusing to ride by a certain landmark that reminds you of it. If these were things that you more than routinely avoided, you might use this practice to imagine yourself, in clear detail, confronting each of these activities with more adaptive responses. Acceptance will help you alter your relationship with whatever it is you fear.

3. Observe your feelings, thoughts, and bodily sensations while you imagine confronting your fear.

Do this once or twice a day for a week, and using a journal or notepad or tracking worksheet available at the website for this book, track how your thoughts, feelings, and bodily sensations differ each time. Try to extend the time you spend with this practice by at least a couple of minutes every day.

Exercise 3.2: **Confront Your Anxiety with Mindfulness in Real Life** Using the tools we have presented in this chapter, plan to practice mindfully confronting your anxiety. For example, if you fear talking on the phone, plan to mindfully call a friend—that is, be fully engaged with the conversation and the purpose of the activity. Or, if you fear enclosed spaces, practice approaching a tight space that you have recently avoided. You may also want to use the object or situation you identified from the previous practice, especially if it's something you are actively trying to overcome. Once you have identified your behavioral target and planned your exposure, choose a specific day and time and follow through with your exposure. Mindfully rate your levels of distress before, during, and after the exposure, and summarize one or two things you learned from the experience (you can use the worksheet at http://www.new harbinger.com/34169). Do this once a day for a week, and track how your thoughts, feelings, and bodily sensations differ each time. Also consider extending the length of your mindfulness practice each time. Keep in mind that the amount of time is less important than devoting a meaningful amount of time to each exercise. For example, if you were to practice being in an enclosed space, such as an elevator, the first time you try it you might only be able to tolerate staying in the elevator for 4 seconds. The next time, however, it would be appropriate to try to increase your tolerance by staying in the elevator for a second or two longer. If you were mindfully confronting a fear of talking on the phone, you might increase the length of time you talk on the phone by a minute or two each day. Essentially, the amount of time by which you increase your practices should be relative to your ability to tolerate the anxiety.

chapter 4

Thinking Traps

Because emotion regulation is one of the core topics of this book, it's important that you examine how you can use certain thinking styles to regulate your emotions. The way you think is often linked to the way you feel. In some instances, you may fall prey to certain thinking traps that cause you to respond to your emotions in unhelpful ways. Such thinking traps are at the root of anxious emotions and, thus, deserve special focus. In this chapter, we will examine the consequences of different thinking styles on emotional expression and how mindfulness can rescue you from unproductive thinking styles.

Different Thinking Styles

So far in this book, we have discussed several models of emotions, which emphasize different action tendencies that are motivated by various kinds of feelings. In recent years, research psychologists have dedicated more and more attention to learning about how people react to emotions, or their *response styles*. This concept refers to individual differences in the way people respond to negative and positive emotions and the overall usefulness of each type of response pattern. Although we briefly mentioned this concept in the introduction, it's worth elaborating on, because response style plays a crucial role in the overall course and development of a given emotion.

Response styles can include any number of specific emotion regulation procedures. For instance, if you feel sad or down, you might distract yourself with music, problem solve by figuring out what you can do to make yourself happy, or even dwell on the causes and meaning of your depression. Whereas the first two techniques might provide some critical distance and facilitate more positive emotions, the last strategy is likely to maintain your negative feelings. Besides resulting in different outcomes, individual response styles are instances of higher-level processes. In other words, different kinds of specific emotion regulation strategies can be organized into broader categories. In this chapter, we will discuss one of the most unhelpful categories: repetitive negative thinking.

It might be helpful to illustrate these concepts with some examples. Let's have a look at Robert and his way of dealing with his fears and distress. Throughout his whole life, Robert has considered himself a socially anxious introvert. When entering conversations, he often doesn't know what to say and fumbles over his words to such an extent that he becomes overly concerned with how others perceive him. Group situations are the worst, because it feels as if he is forced to enter a competition he has no hope of winning. Everyone else seems to exchange jokes and witty comments with nonchalance and ease. Robert, on the other hand, remains petrified, because his heart flutters whenever he attempts to muster enough courage to make any sort of comment whatsoever.

In certain situations, his anxiety can reach such a level that he feels as if he might have a panic attack! When required to give a presentation in front of his team members for his job, he spends days and days worrying about all the things that could go wrong. There have been times when he became so sensitive to his emotional arousal and pounding heart that he experienced a panic attack minutes before having to give a presentation. Afterward, he spent days ruminating on his performance and moping about his inability to do anything.

Robert's typical style of dealing with negative emotions contributes to the overall course of his anxiety. For instance, prior to going to a party, he spends countless hours anticipating the horrible things that could happen in this social situation. His worrying becomes difficult to control, as certain thoughts persist in his mind. On one hand, this constant form of mental preparation makes Robert feel as if he is doing something productive that will enable him to better survive the party, but on the other hand, it reinforces his belief that the party is a dangerous situation that has social costs. (This is exactly the kind of future-oriented anxiety and worry we described in chapter 1.) Moreover, he worries *during* the party as well. Being preoccupied throughout the party with thoughts of what might happen next takes him away from present-moment interactions and social exchanges.

Also, Robert feels the need to analyze his "performance" after the party. He might recall that during one conversation he was breathing more rapidly than usual. Furthermore, he considers his accelerated breathing a sign of anxiety and of his inability to cope with social encounters. Negative interpretations are given to relatively normal occurrences, which turn into signals of threat and danger. This is not uncommon in social anxiety disorder. In fact, researchers use the term *post-event rumination* to describe when people dwell on perceived social failures in an attempt to avoid them in future. This strategy often maintains anxiety and encourages people to interpret their performance as unsatisfactory and a source of embarrassment.

Now let's take a step back. What do all of Robert's response styles have in common? Can you come up with some adjectives to describe how he has been approaching his emotions? One immediately noticeable characteristic of his response style is its negativity. Before a social event, he focuses on what might go badly rather than on what might go well. After a social event, rarely does Robert reflect on successful encounters. Instead, he rehashes encounters in which he felt uncomfortable.

Second, his response style is repetitive and cyclical. He doesn't devote a discrete amount of time to responding to his negative emotions; he wallows in them for hours on end. Spending large amounts of time on his emotions seems productive, as if he's getting to the bottom of what's going on. But when his thoughts take on this negative, judgmental nature, Robert is doing more harm than good. No amount of brooding will foster the courage and confidence necessary to outsmart anxiety. Instead, mentally replaying uncomfortable encounters reinforces the idea that his emotions are unruly and uncontrollable.

Can you think of any other distinguishing characteristics of Robert's response style? This third one is slightly trickier. His response style is *cognitive* in nature. A response style isn't an emotion; it's a thought or belief that influences the form, development, and course of your emotional experience. Often processes such as worry and rumination are verbal in nature. When people worry about the future, they often try to analyze all the bad things that could happen in sentence form (for example, *If I were to request an extension on this deadline, my boss would be disappointed in me.*). The verbal nature of worrying prevents people from actually imagining these circumstances in a more vividly visual form. Essentially, rather than experiencing some unwanted future event as a realistic and lively image, people will try to take the edge off by using language that is more detached, analytical, and subdued. Although this initially sounds like a very appealing strategy, it serves as a way of avoiding intense emotional experiences and teaches you that your future circumstances, as well as the unpleasant emotions that accompany them, are dangerous.

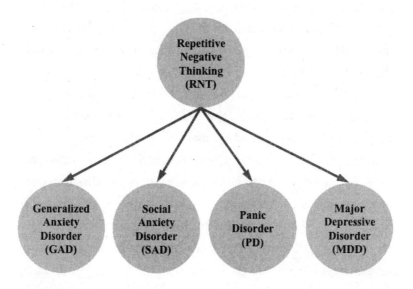

Figure 4.1. Model of Repetitive Negative Thinking and Clinical Disorders

Combining these three elements gives us the name of this response style: *repetitive negative thinking.* Can you identify any times during your own life when you used this approach? Repetitive negative thinking can be detrimental and is common in many forms of anxiety. In the next section, we will further explore its relationship with anxiety.

Repetitive Negative Thinking and Anxiety

Anxiety comes in many forms. In fact, the fifth edition of the *Diagnostic and Statistical Manual of Mental Disorders* (DSM-5) recognizes several anxiety conditions, including generalized anxiety disorder, social anxiety disorder, panic disorder, and specific phobias. Anxiety doesn't fall neatly into these categories, however. Many of the symptoms of different anxiety conditions overlap, which can make diagnosis difficult. Another important fact about anxiety disorders is that they have very high rates of comorbidity—that is, they often co-occur (Kessler et al. 2005, using *DSM-IV* criteria). Furthermore, these disorders aren't set in stone. For example, a person who has high levels of social anxiety can eventually begin to predominantly experience symptoms of generalized anxiety disorder. Anxiety disorders can even morph into depressive disorders and other forms of distress. As a result of the difficulties inherent in the diagnosis of anxiety disorders and their high levels of comorbidity, researchers have invested a great deal of effort in coming up with reasonable explanations of this phenomenon. The search for *transdiagnostic factors,* or maladaptive processes that are common to and underlie different types of anxiety, has become increasingly relevant. Emotion dysregulation and harmful response styles have been considered potential transdiagnostic factors. For now, we will focus on repetitive negative thinking as a core feature found across different types of anxiety.

Repetitive Negative Thinking and Generalized Anxiety Disorder (GAD)

The cardinal symptom of GAD is uncontrollable, excessive worry. Many theories have conceptualized worry as a verbal thought process that temporarily dampens distressing emotions and the threatening imagery associated with future threats. Contemporary models of GAD and worry suggest that individuals with GAD use worry not only to avoid negative emotions but also to mitigate *contrasts* between emotions (Newman et al. 2013). Specifically, individuals with GAD try to avoid contrasts between initial positive emotions and later negative emotions. In an experiment conducted by Llera and Newman (2014), participants with GAD and participants without any form of anxiety were randomly assigned to experience worrisome, relaxing, or neutral thoughts before watching scary, sad, or humorous film clips. Essentially, the researchers wanted to know the effect of using different emotion regulation strategies on experiencing an emotional contrast. Indeed, when individuals with GAD used worry before being exposed to scary or sad film clips, they felt more prepared for the upcoming emotional threat. Because they had been worrying, they were already in a negative state. The scary or sad film clip could thus do little to make them feel worse. On the other hand, when they didn't use worry and were thus in a neutral emotional state, they perceived the scary or sad film clip to be more distressing. The overall results of the study indicated that those with GAD considered worry to be a useful coping strategy for dealing with drastic changes from positive to negative experiences, whereas nonanxious individuals did not consider worry a useful strategy. This may explain why many individuals describe worry as useful or productive. However, we know that prolonged use of worry actually leads to more anxiety and prevents people from realizing that experiencing negative emotions and emotional contrasts isn't all that bad.

Repetitive Negative Thinking and Social Anxiety Disorder (SAD)

We already talked about Robert and his experience with SAD, and this gives us a good template for exploring the role of repetitive negative thinking in social anxiety. Like GAD, SAD is associated with anticipatory worry about upcoming social interactions or performance situations. People often rehearse what might go wrong, focus on how others might perceive their performance, and try to predict how they might feel during different circumstances of the interaction. In addition to worry, there has been increasing evidence that those with SAD also engage in post-event rumination. As we mentioned earlier, this refers to a process in which socially anxious individuals scrutinize their performance after the fact. They try to determine how others perceived them, whether anyone noticed their perceived social blunders, and what their anxiety means about them as a person. In an experiment by Penney and Abbott (2015), individuals with or without SAD underwent a threatening speech task in which they were held to very high standards. The researchers examined what participants were thinking and feeling throughout the whole experiment. The results revealed that those with SAD engaged in post-event rumination to a greater extent than did those without SAD. Furthermore, the more threatening the participants perceived the speech task to be, the more they ruminated. Even though anxiety is often a future-oriented experience, repetitive negative thinking can both precede and follow threatening events or situations.

Repetitive Negative Thinking and Panic Disorder (PD)

Imagine experiencing the most intense surge of fear you have ever felt. It causes a psychological and physical reaction that affects your whole body. When anxiety reaches such an extreme, some people think they are having a heart attack! These episodes of anxiety, also known as panic attacks, consist of accelerated heart rate, difficulty breathing, trembling hands, fear of losing control, and even out-of-body experiences.

Panic attacks can occur in many different anxiety disorders, but some people experience them out of the blue on a frequent basis. When this happens, a diagnosis of panic disorder (PD) might be assigned. One of the key features of PD is prolonged worry about when the next panic attack might occur and what the panic attacks might mean. In one study (Cucchi et al. 2012), people experiencing PD and nonanxious individuals were administered a variety of assessments, including measures that appraised their reasons for worrying. It was found that, compared with nonanxious individuals, people who experience panic attacks tend to have more negative beliefs about the uncontrollability and danger of worry and feel a greater need to be in control of their worry. This has important implications. Attempts to exercise more control over one's worry, and beliefs that one's thoughts are uncontrollable, create a disastrous cycle of conflict. Often people's motives for using maladaptive emotion regulation strategies lead to unintended consequences that end up causing more harm than good. By feeling the need to exercise more control over worry, people will try to rigidly suppress worrying, which actually backfires by causing more negative thoughts and anxiety.

Repetitive Negative Thinking and Major Depressive Disorder (MDD)

Though not an anxiety disorder, MDD is often comorbid with anxiety. In fact, comorbidity between anxiety and depressive disorders is the rule rather than the exception. Because of this, several researchers have investigated repetitive negative thinking across both of these disorders and amassed a large body of evidence that supports repetitive negative thinking as the process that links them. In one study (Drost et al. 2014), people diagnosed with anxiety and depressive disorders were assessed for several years. The researchers measured such things as symptoms of anxiety, symptoms of low mood and depression, rumination, and worry. Their pattern of results provided a very consistent picture of how MDD interacts with anxiety disorders. In short, they found that repetitive negative thinking was the reason why people with high levels of depression experience greater levels of anxiety in later years. This proved to be the case in the opposite direction as well, as repetitive negative thinking made anxious people experience more symptoms of depression in later years. Therefore, it appears as if repetitive negative thinking can help explain why people with significant anxiety often undergo periods of depression later on in life.

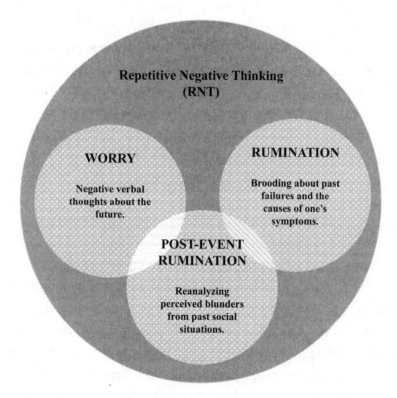

Figure 4.2. Different Types of Repetitive Negative Thinking

By now, you have seen how repetitive negative thinking plays a crucial role across various expressions of anxiety. When reviewing the evidence, it's easy to understand why separate anxiety disorders often occur together, because they share a considerable number of features. This overlap has very important consequences. Namely, if there was a way to target repetitive negative thinking, it could alleviate a wide variety of anxious symptoms so that people wouldn't have to undergo specific treatments for each disorder. Well, we are in luck! Recent years have witnessed many compelling studies that corroborated techniques based on mindfulness and emotion regulation as effective strategies for counteracting repetitive negative thinking. In the next section, we will detail procedures and specific exercises that have been scientifically proven to help people outsmart repetitive negative thinking and anxiety.

A Nonjudgmental Approach to Repetitive Negative Thinking

By now, it should come as no surprise that the very same mindfulness-based approaches you learned in the last two chapters can help you regulate your emotions effectively. This proves especially true in the case of repetitive negative thinking. As evidenced by its name, repetitive negative thinking entails prolonged periods of negative, overly pessimistic, and judgmental thinking. Whether you are reliving past disasters or imagining future ones, repetitive negative thinking can easily remove you from the present. Do you remember times when you exhausted yourself worrying about some impending situation that inspired dread and uncertainty? For instance, it's common to worry about a very important exam that could have a big impact on your future (such as the SAT or GRE). Or do you recall times when you became especially concerned about some past mishap and how its consequences might affect you? Many people think about former romances and what led to the eventual breakup. When you engage in repetitive negative thinking, you are directing your attention to a world that exists only in your mind, a world fraught with fearful circumstances. As we have seen, mindfulness can foster a greater sense of present awareness, enabling you to savor life experiences that are happening now.

Combating repetitive negative thinking can be tough. It's incredibly difficult to let go of thinking about something that you perceive as dangerous or distressing. After all, when you adopt repetitive negative thinking as a means of handling anxiety, you do so likely because you believe it will somehow prove beneficial. Worrying feels a lot like problem solving—you are exploring every facet of an uncertain predicament in order to obtain some sense of closure. Yet prolonged worry can have devastating consequences. First, it prevents you from actually facing the emotion or circumstance that you perceive as threatening. As we mentioned earlier in this chapter, worry has an avoidance function that prevents you from actually learning whether the uncertainty of the future is all that bad. Second, worrying takes you away from the present moment by forcing you to focus on the future. This can diminish the quality of your everyday experiences. Third, worrying is both cyclical and negative, which means that it's hard to just "turn off" the process by suppressing your thoughts.

With practice, however, you can achieve mastery over your thoughts and overcome the unwelcome presence of repetitive negative thinking. What follows are some mindfulness-based practices for targeting common thinking traps that lead to repetitive negative thinking.

Outsmarting Anxiety Skill #3:
Avoid common thinking traps.

Suggested Practices

Before you begin to implement these practices, review the guidelines we provided in chapter 2. It's important that you be consistent and patient. Practice daily, and be forgiving of yourself if you make a mistake—for example, if you become distracted by an occasional worry or accidentally think of something judgmentally.

Some mindfulness and meditation techniques emphasize concentrating on the present moment without focusing on any particular object. When dealing with repetitive negative thinking, however, attempts to move your focus away from negative thoughts often can be met with more intrusive worries. The negative thoughts can feel omnipresent and consuming. In this case, it might be helpful to focus on something that will facilitate nonjudgmental mindfulness, yet something it's impossible to leave home without so that you can use it anywhere and anytime. Can you think of something that's always with you, no matter what? Your breath!

The use of breathing techniques as a means of meditation has a long history in the practice of mindfulness. Because breathing is something you do so often it has become second nature, it's unlikely that you have spent much time thinking about what it feels like; thus, mindfulness of your breath also provides you with a good opportunity to get yourself out of automatic pilot mode and achieve present-moment awareness.

Exercise 4.1: **The Nonjudgmental Breath**   For the next three minutes, take a moment to pause. During this time, direct all of your consciousness and attention to your breathing. Approach your breath with openness and genuine interest. Do your best to notice aspects of your breathing you have never thought about before. For instance, take a moment to register the qualitative experience of breathing. What does it feel like to inhale, hold your breath, and then exhale? Is the air warm or cold? Try alternating between breathing through your nose and breathing through your mouth. Do you notice any differences?

The most important part of this exercise is to simply acknowledge and note the different experiences without evaluating them. Nothing is inherently good or bad about a particular breath you take. It's just a process that your body performs, and it's fine to leave it at that.

During this practice, sometimes you may notice that your mind has wandered to repetitive negative thoughts. It doesn't mean you did anything wrong, and it's entirely natural. What you do with these thoughts, however, will determine your eventual emotional condition. So try to take the same nonjudgmental attitude toward any worrisome thoughts you have as you are taking toward your breathing. There's no need to appraise a worrisome thought as good or bad. It's simply a thought, which is a natural mental occurrence, just as breathing is a natural physical occurrence. Patiently redirect your consciousness to your breathing while noting that you had a thought.

Noticing when your attention has wandered and redirecting it nonjudgmentally to your breath will require some practice, but continued use of this exercise will be of long-term benefit. Furthermore, you can do it at any time and in just about any context. Your surroundings may change, but using your breathing as a focal point for your nonjudgmental consciousness will enable you to apply this mind-set across a wide variety of situations.

Repetitive negative thinking can feel like a never-ending chain of thoughts. As soon as one worry appears, it can give rise to other concerns that preoccupy your attention and remove you from the present. For instance, you might worry about meeting a deadline for a project at work. These thoughts might prompt you to worry about something else. Sometimes people even worry about their worry: they become conscious of the worries themselves and feel the need to control them, which, in turn, becomes a cause of concern.

Now, let us see how we can use mindfulness to counteract the exhausting effects of repetitive negative thinking. If you have been practicing the *nonreactive stance* taught in chapter 2, then you are already halfway there, because fostering a nonreactive, mindful disposition is the healthy opposite of repetitive negative thinking. In chapter 2, we invited you to look at an object and notice its color, texture, weight, and dimensions in a nonreactive manner. In the following practice, we will invite you to look at something of your own imagining: a worst-case scenario.

When such scenarios come to mind, your normal reaction may be to worry in an effort to determine how you can prevent them. This time, however, you will practice not reacting. The goal of this exercise is for you to create upsetting mental images without feeling as if you need to do anything about them. This will be difficult to accomplish on the first try! The key is to approach distressing thoughts with an attitude of total acceptance rather than reactivity.

Exercise 4.2: **Accept, Don't React**   Consider the sorts of things you worry about, and contemplate a worst-case scenario. As an example, if you have social anxiety, imagine that you have to give a presentation to a committee. Picture what it would be like if your mind went blank, preventing you from finishing your presentation and provoking laughter among the committee members. As embarrassing and uncomfortable as the thought may be, confront it. Don't shrink from it. Instead of reacting to this fearful thought and feeling a need to worry about how you might do better, simply accept that you are having a fearful thought. If you find yourself reacting to the distress your imaginings cause and engaging in repetitive negative thinking, you can recompose yourself by accepting your thoughts, feelings, and inclinations without ascribing any particular meaning to them. By so doing, you will be regulating your emotions mindfully.

Another reason why repetitive negative thinking is repetitive in nature is because people never really feel satisfied that they worried or ruminated enough. Usually worry and rumination are undertaken with some purpose in mind. People often believe that if they worry enough about something happening, then they will be better equipped to handle their emotions if it really happens. But that's the main catch with repetitive negative thinking: how much worrying is *enough*? Despite people's intentions, they often fail to achieve the sense of satisfaction and closure they desire at the outset. The lack of clearness about when it's appropriate to stop worrying leads to an out-of-control spiral of negative thinking.

Exercise 4.3: **Postpone Your Worries**   Set aside a fifteen-minute period every evening in which you do nothing but worry. Then, if at any other time of day you think you have reason to worry, instead of mentally addressing the problem on the spot, just leave it alone and tell yourself that you will deal with it during your *worry* *period.* If you are contending with the pressures and vicissitudes of work, remind yourself that you can engage with your worries during your worry period. There's no need to worry immediately. Mentally note that you have experienced a *worry trigger* by stating to yourself: *I have experienced a distressing thought, but it's nothing more than just that: a thought. I can always return to it during my worry period tonight.*

If you practice this often enough, you may no longer feel the need to address your worries once the worry period arrives. Furthermore, this technique promotes mindfulness, which loosens the grip of distressing thoughts because you no longer feel as if you have to identify with them.

⁘

This chapter has hopefully added to your understanding of anxiety by introducing repetitive negative thinking. Different response styles, or ways you think about your emotions, will have different effects on the overall expression and development of your emotions. We illustrated that specific forms of emotion dysregulation, such as worry, rumination, and post-event rumination, all share the common features that make up repetitive negative thinking. Moreover, we demonstrated how the use of mindfulness provides a way of engaging with emotions that avoids the pitfalls of repetitive negative thinking. Unlike repetitive negative thinking, mindfulness encourages a nonreactive, nonjudgmental approach toward fear and other anxious emotions. Rather than having your attention be diverted to negative aspects of the future or past with intrusive worries, mindfulness-based techniques allow you to enjoy the here and now. Remember, with enough practice, anyone can benefit from the techniques discussed in this chapter. Using mindfulness to counteract repetitive negative thinking is an important step toward mastering your anxiety.

chapter 5

Emotional Inflexibility

Can you remember a time you got into a heated argument and ending up fighting for a position you didn't necessarily agree with, just because you felt as if you couldn't change course? This sort of thing can happen to everyone at some point, but sometimes people have difficulties letting go of a certain emotion. It takes a lot of effort to reassess your situation and detach from what you were feeling before, especially in the case of anxiety. As we highlighted before, anxiety is cyclical and repetitive in nature, which makes it very difficult for people with anxiety to be flexible in responding to their emotions. In this chapter, we will take a look at how emotional inflexibility can influence anxiety and ways to overcome this.

Trying to Control Your Emotions

People often experience anxiety as something that's unwanted and involuntary. It's not as if people have a keen desire to feel nervous or threatened. In many ways, excessive anxiety can be thought of as an unwanted house guest. We will discuss two different ways of dealing with this "houseguest."

One option is to exercise rigid control over your anxiety. This can give the impression that you are the one in charge. By just shutting anxiety out of your life with that special combination of willpower and effort, your problem will be solved, and you can return to a normal life. The problem with this strategy is that scientific research shows it doesn't necessarily work. As we will discuss a little later, such attempts can often backfire.

The less stringent path is to approach your emotions in a more flexible manner. By accepting your emotional experience as something that doesn't require an immediate response, you will place yourself in a better position. Emotions naturally ebb and flow on their own. Adaptiveness and flexibility are key to fostering a healthy relationship with anxiety.

As we will demonstrate in the second half of this chapter, flexibility and inflexibility represent two general rubrics under which several distinct processes lie. But for now, it will be helpful to discuss this in a broader framework. As discussed earlier, emotions emerge as a consequence of events. For example, your boss informs you that he will have to consider layoffs in the near future; as a result, you feel worry and concern. On the other hand, you may be delighted to learn that a close friend will be visiting you next weekend. Emotions are contextual in nature, corresponding to an external situation that elicits them. Being able to flexibly adapt your emotions in relation to environmental demands is a hallmark of mental health. Anguish and distress often occur when certain emotions are inappropriately applied to situations that don't warrant them. Can you think of any examples of inflexible responding?

Earlier, we described repetitive negative thinking, such as worry and rumination, which can lead to increases in anxiety, depression, and other negative mind-sets. Consider what happens when people worry frequently and uncontrollably about future occurrences: they are experiencing emotions that aren't appropriate to whatever is going on around them. They are feeling, under nonthreatening circumstances, the distress that would befit a worst-case scenario. This is why habitual worriers are often portrayed as distracted people who are too lost in their own thoughts to enjoy the company of others or to appreciate the small things in life (think of Woody Allen's neurotic persona in cinema). As you can see, inflexibility can result in some unfortunate consequences.

Responding to and Managing Your Emotions

We have seen what inflexibility looks like, but what might emotional flexibility entail? Well, for one thing, it requires more than attempts to exude positivity at all times. Sometimes emotions many people consider ugly and unproductive have a function. When anger is directed in the right way and in the right context, it can become a statement against injustice. Consider the causes for which activists fight and how they channel frustration into progress. Therefore, it's important that you be able to adapt your emotions to your current situation.

When it comes to fear and anxiety, try to remember that these are often future-oriented emotions. The pounding heart, the hypervigilant mind—they manifest in response to an imminent threat. The illusion of threat can arise easily for those who are predisposed to perceive danger and misfortune at every turn. You can use mindfulness-based techniques to do the healthy opposite: become immersed in the present! When you are more focused in the present moment, you are more attuned to your *environmental demands*. By this, we mean the ups and downs of your daily life that require certain emotional responses for you to engage with your environment effectively. At a party, for example, feeling relaxed and content would be most conducive to having a good time. Likewise, at work, being focused and interested in your project would be best for your productivity. What worry does is remove you from the present moment and transport you to a world fraught with distress, uncertainty, and threat.

So all you have to do is figure out what emotion is best suited to your present-moment circumstances and then try to adopt that emotion. It seems so easy, right? Well, it can be difficult to do by force of will alone. Our main strategy to help you accomplish this kind of flexibility is mindfulness.

Mindfulness is a great way to become centered in the present moment. In fact, it might even be a link between flexibility and less anxiety. In one of our own studies (Curtiss and Klemanski 2014a), we attempted to determine why psychological flexibility is associated with fewer symptoms of anxiety and depression. We administered several psychological assessments to various people who were diagnosed with clinical levels of anxiety or depression. Essentially, we found that very specific facets of mindfulness were responsible for this link, and two models of psychological flexibility emerged. In the first model, we looked at the relationship between psychological flexibility and anxiety, and we found that nonreactivity explained why increased psychological flexibility was related to fewer anxiety symptoms. Increases in psychological flexibility led to increases in nonreactivity, which, in turn, were related to decreases in anxiety. We found a somewhat similar pattern of results in the second model. It appears that nonjudgment explained the relationship between psychological flexibility and depression. Specifically, increases in psychological flexibility led to increases in nonjudgment, which then led to decreases in depressive symptoms. Therefore, we will now teach you some additional mindfulness techniques that will bolster the skills you have acquired thus far.

Outsmarting Anxiety Skill #4:
Flexibly respond to your emotions.

Suggested Practices

Before you begin the following practices, remember that it's important to be consistent and patient. Practice daily, and be forgiving with yourself if you make a mistake! These techniques are meant to help you be mindful and flexible "on the go."

Even though we already presented the basics of mindfulness, it's important that you keep up your practice throughout the day. As we have mentioned before, mindfulness is a mind-set, and you need to "exercise" regularly throughout the day to maintain this state of mental health. Although it might be easy to practice meditation at scheduled times in places that are free from distraction, how exactly are you supposed to meditate while walking in the grocery store, driving on the highway, or working in the office? Well, even if you can't get a full course of meditation in, you can practice the basics in just about any situation.

The first technique involves counting, which you can practice in at least two different ways. Building on what you learned in chapter 4, you know that meditation lets you be more in tune with the present moment. And present-moment awareness, as you have learned in this chapter, makes it more likely that your emotional responses will be appropriate to your surroundings. Recall that we described how non-judgmentally paying attention to your breath fosters mindfulness.

Exercise 5.1: **Counting Meditation**   Counting meditation allows you to practice the basics of mindfulness in situations that are often very distracting and not conducive to sustained focus. If it seems difficult, be patient and persevere. After a time, you will consider it much easier to achieve mindfulness in these everyday situations and therefore be more flexible in your emotional responses because you will have greater awareness of the present than of concerns about the future. Here are two types of counting meditation.

Counting Breaths

For approximately thirty seconds, count the number of breaths you take. Try to really focus on how the number sounds as you say it silently to yourself. You can count sequentially (*One, two, three…*), or you can count up to a certain number and then start over (for example, *One, two, one, two…*). This latter technique is recommended in case you become too concerned about what number is next in your sequential count.

The next time you are at work, try to practice breath-counting for thirty seconds once an hour or in conjunction with something you do regularly, such as checking your e-mail. You will notice that it gets easier with practice and that you will feel more grounded in the present moment.

Counting Steps

Count your steps as you walk. This works best in places such as grocery stores or when you are going for long walks. You will notice that your counting is much quicker during walking than during breathing, but still try to keep your attention engrossed in your steps. Again, depending on your own preference, you may find it helpful to count sequentially or in repeated blocks for thirty seconds.

Some forms of mindfulness encourage people to encounter an object with curiosity, lovingness, and appreciation. If you have given counting meditation a chance, then you may like to complement it with the following spin-off, called *hand appreciation*. Because your hands are such familiar and common parts of your body, they are an excellent object for meditative focus.

Exercise 5.2: **Give Yourself a Helping Hand**   Visually explore your hand with a sense of novelty and curiosity. Pretend you have never seen a hand before, trying to forget all of your preconceptions of what a hand is for. Spend fifteen seconds on each hand. Explore your hand's crevices and follow them as they intersect with other lines. Note the patterns and contemplate them without judgment, without reference to the fact that these are familiar objects, and without reaction. By fostering a *genuine*, rather than pretended, curiosity about something as commonplace as your hands, you are training yourself to focus on the present moment even when

it seems tedious or boring. And what does present-moment awareness help with? Emotional flexibility! By forgoing the urge to
remove yourself to a future filled with worry, you will be in a better
position to gauge what emotions are most appropriate in your surrounding environment.

⁂

So far, we have presented the fundamentals of flexible and
inflexible emotion regulation. As we have seen, inflexible
response styles are rigid and unhelpful; they give rise to
emotions that are inappropriate because the situation
doesn't call for them. Furthermore, we have learned how
these on-the-go mindfulness techniques will help you cultivate flexibility by being more aware of the present moment.
Next, we will take these concepts and skills one step further
by exploring specific facets of inflexibility and specific techniques that will enable you to overcome them.

Specific Strategies for Flexibly Regulating Your Emotions

In the first part of this chapter, we explained *how* to respond
to and manage your anxious emotions by using a flexible
approach. We will now review specific types of emotion regulation strategies that teach you *what* to do (and what not to
do!) to modify the intensity and magnitude of your emotional experiences. By combining these approaches to managing your emotions, you will be better equipped to flexibly
and adaptively implement strategies that correspond to both
the demands of your environment and your internal mood
state.

To experience life at all requires a certain amount of vulnerability to your emotions. Emotions play a crucial role in everyday life, whether they entail reveling in time spent with family, grieving when you lose someone from your life, or feeling scared or intimidated in an unfamiliar situation. Emotions not only provide you with context about your experiences but also help you appropriately respond to the demands of a particular situation. In essence, emotions serve a specific function, or purpose, in terms of the meaning they give to your life and the responses they elicit. For example, your emotions can help you make decisions quickly (or help you know when you should take your time), prepare your body's physiological processes for immediate action, influence your thoughts and secondary emotions, motivate your future behavior, and help you communicate.

Imagine negotiating with a salesperson the price of a car you want to buy. If during the negotiation you suddenly feel uneasy about the deal being offered, an emotion is likely motivating you to further evaluate the situation. For example, perhaps you have a notion that the salesperson is trying to take advantage of you, or maybe you are worried that the price of the car exceeds your budget. Regardless of your interpretation, your emotion serves as a cue for you to take action and provides relevance to your concerns. It essentially prompts you to modify the relationship you have to your environment (in this scenario, you could impulsively take the deal, hastily walk away, or cautiously ask for some time to fully consider the offer).

Emotions can be quite powerful, and it's easy to feel as if you have no control over them. The good news is that emotions can be managed, but managing them correctly and flexibly requires a considerable deal of effort and practice.

When managed correctly, emotions will work in your favor and lead to adaptive and healthy responses, especially in anxiety-provoking situations. Conversely, when emotions are managed poorly (or not at all), they can lead to maladaptive behaviors that foster anxiety and even depression.

Practice   What cues do you receive from various emotions? For example, what actions might joy and happiness lead to in your everyday life? Perhaps you would be more open to meeting new people or engaging in new experiences. How about anger? For some, anger might create a sense of control through assertive communication or problem solving; for others, it might signal a need to be alone and reflect on the problem at hand. Consider the cues you receive from happiness, anger, anxiety, contentment, desire, disgust, fear, sadness, surprise, and other emotions.

Adaptive and Maladaptive Emotion Regulation Strategies

Emotion regulation refers to both *what* you do to modulate your emotions in response to your environment and *how*. By employing various emotion regulation strategies, you can modify any of the following:

- Situations that elicit emotions

- The type of emotion you experience

- The intensity and magnitude of your emotional response

For example, imagine that while you are riding in an elevator, the elevator suddenly stops, the lights go out, and the doors won't open. After several seconds, once you realize you are truly stuck, you feel anxious and on the verge of panic. You frantically push buttons (not helpful!), scan the ceiling for an escape route (more dangerous!), and try to pry open the steel doors (not going to happen!). Your emotions in this situation cue you to take action to try to change the situation; however, despite your best efforts, you remain stuck. In a moment of surprising clarity, you realize that feeling anxious is going to get in the way of thinking clearly and remaining calm. To try to change your emotion altogether, you might try to talk to others in the elevator or, if you are by yourself, pass the time by doing something productive or positive (such as watching funny videos on your smartphone or organizing your bag or purse). If those strategies don't work, you then might try to simply lower your anxiety by taking time to relax, breathe deeply, or more realistically appraise the situation (for example, *People are working to help get me out of the elevator. I won't be in here forever.*).

Psychologists who study emotion have focused on understanding the nature of various emotion regulation strategies in terms of their adaptiveness. More specifically, *adaptive emotion regulation* refers to particular strategies that are helpful for effectively managing emotions and that reduce the risk of anxiety disorders. In the elevator scenario above, reducing the intensity of your emotional experience through relaxation and deep breathing are examples of adaptive emotion regulation responses—that is, they both help you remain calm and make sensible decisions while in the elevator. *Maladaptive strategies,* on the other hand, are generally thought to be less helpful and potentially detrimental to your well-being (frantically pushing buttons or trying to escape out of the ceiling hatch, for example, will probably do you more harm than good). Indeed, research has shown that increased use of adaptive emotion regulation strategies is associated with lower rates of anxiety and depression, whereas maladaptive strategies are thought to potentially cause several psychiatric disorders and maintain them over time (Aldao and Nolen-Hoeksema 2010).

Adaptive Emotion Regulation

Several types of adaptive emotion regulation skills have been shown to be especially helpful for managing anxiety across of a variety of situations and contexts. These include *reappraisal, problem solving, acceptance,* and *decentering.* Although these strategies might seem fairly straightforward or easy to implement, they all require effort and practice, *especially during times of anxiety.*

REAPPRAISAL

If you were thinking about selling something valuable, such as a home or a prized collection, you likely would want to know how much someone might be willing to pay for it. To estimate its value, you might hire someone to appraise its worth. If you didn't agree with the appraiser's assessment, you might ask him or her to reevaluate. When it comes to emotions, it's often helpful to use a similar approach, especially when the emotion is problematic or has proven too difficult to manage.

Reappraisal, or reinterpreting, entails generating neutral or positive interpretations of the relationship you have to a feared object or situation. It alters the emotional significance of a situation by changing the way you think about your ability to manage the demands of a situation. When used correctly and in appropriate contexts, reappraisal typically results in positive emotional and physiological responses (Gross 1998). For example, you may think that traveling by plane is inherently more dangerous than traveling by car, especially because plane crashes tend to be more catastrophic and newsworthy than car crashes. However, the risk of being in an automobile accident is vastly higher than the risk of being in an airplane accident. The calculated lifetime risk of dying in a motor vehicle accident is 1 in 112, whereas the risk of dying in a commercial airplane crash is 1 in 96,566 (National Safety Council 2015). Reappraising the situation once you know the relative safety of air travel may help you regulate your anxiety and allow you to feel more at ease while flying. Alternatively, you could try to reappraise your thoughts about your ability to manage the demands imposed on you by flying (for example, thinking that you are capable of managing your emotions while flying).

Practice　Take a moment to identify two or three current fears, worries, or stressors. Now, try your best to reframe each situation by identifying a positive or neutral aspect of the situation. For example, if you recently had an argument with a family member, instead of dwelling on the content of the argument, use this as an opportunity to identify ways to improve your communication or think about how to avoid such an argument in the future. If it's difficult to reappraise a particular event or situation, imagine how you might view your current anxiety a year from now or think of how things might be worse (for example, times may be tough, but you likely aren't going hungry, you have a roof over your head, and you have access to health care). This should give you some distance from your current problems, allowing your perspective to shift.

PROBLEM SOLVING

Problem solving as a response to your emotions, such as devising solutions or planning a course of action, represents a conscious effort to change a difficult situation or contain its consequences (in other words, perform damage control). Problem solving benefits your emotions by modifying or eliminating stressors, which, in turn, reduces emotional reactivity. For instance, imagine that you have become anxious and stressed about work, so much so that you dread going to work each day. Rather than thinking that your negative emotional response to work is the problem, it would be better to identify the problem (for example, a colleague is trying to sabotage your work, or your boss is too demanding) and address it by generating solutions and taking the most appropriate course of action.

ACCEPTANCE

Acceptance, as an emotion regulation strategy, dictates that you fully acknowledge, appreciate, endorse, and support your current reality (Hayes 2004). For example, think about your current job. By going to work each day, you are demonstrating acceptance of your current position in life. One day in the future you may dream of having a higher-paying job with more responsibility and authority, but right now, there are likely advantages to your current job and how it fits into your life. Although it may not be perfect in every way, you still accept it as your current reality and without resistance. Perhaps you will apply for a new job tomorrow, or next week, or even a year from now, but while you are in your current job, you still accept it as part of your life.

Acceptance involves a present-centered awareness in which thoughts, feelings, behaviors, and bodily sensations are accepted as they are and without resistance. In essence, acceptance necessitates that you recognize that life, and its consequences, can't always be controlled. Responding to your emotions with acceptance doesn't imply that you condone your circumstances, but it does allow you to stop fighting reality. In so doing, you are less likely to resist or avoid your emotional experiences, no matter how painful, thereby reducing your personal suffering.

If you have ever found yourself remarking that something is unfair or that something shouldn't be a certain way, it's a sign that you haven't accepted your circumstances or the reality of life. Acceptance can be an incredibly powerful tool, especially during moments of anxiety. For example, if you or a loved one were to receive unfavorable news, you might initially be inclined to refuse to accept the truth. Yet to do so would only add suffering to your pain. Conversely, if you were to accept the news, you would be more capable of confronting your emotions and viewing them as a fleeting experience rather than something that defines you.

Practice Identify something that you are currently having a hard time accepting. Perhaps you have been resisting or fighting some emotional or physical pain, or you have a lot of regret about a past relationship or behavior. No matter what the problem, consider actively practicing acceptance in order to reduce your suffering. Write down the problem you are having trouble accepting, and record the following:

- Thoughts and emotions you experience when you think about the troubling problem or situation

- Behaviors or strategies you use to avoid negative thoughts or unpleasant feelings related to the problem or situation

- The judgments you have about your thoughts, emotions, and behaviors related to the problem

Next, generate strong counterarguments to your judgments, as if you are an opposing lawyer. Choose the strongest counterargument, and practice using this argument each time a negative thought, emotion, or behavior arises when you think about the troubling problem or situation.

Repeat these steps as often as needed to practice acceptance.

DECENTERING

If you are at all familiar with cable television news shows, you have likely noticed that in addition to the frenzied pace of live reports and flashing informational graphics, tickers at the bottom of the screen scroll by with headlines for breaking news, sports scores, and financial news. Imagine trying to pay attention to all the information being presented to you in a single half-hour show. It's virtually impossible and highly impractical; after all, not every news story is important to you.

Our modern environments are similar to these frenzied news programs. In our everyday lives, we must constantly process information from our surroundings and within our own minds. It's easy to become consumed with the numerous thoughts and feelings we experience each day. When this happens, it's difficult to make sense of what we think or how we feel in the midst of our own mental chaos.

To counteract this turmoil, psychologists who study emotion recommend using a regulation strategy known as *decentering*. Decentering refers to the notion that not all thoughts (and feelings) should be clung to as absolute truths; instead, thoughts and feelings should be held more loosely, as objective events (Safran and Segal 1990). More simply, decentering encourages you to quietly witness your thoughts, without judgment, as they pass by. The key idea is to learn that you don't need to believe all of your thoughts, and not all your thoughts are equally important; some are important and should be noticed, but many are born out of irrational ways of thinking or biases that you have developed.

Exercise 5.3: **Watch Your Ships Sail By**   Find a quiet and comfortable place where you can sit upright on a chair (with an unsupported back) or on a cushion on the floor. Adopt a relaxed but alert posture. Once you are seated, set a timer to alert you when five minutes have passed.

For those five minutes, mindfully and nonjudgmentally notice any thoughts, emotions, or sensations that arise. If it helps, imagine yourself watching ships sail by as you sit on the shore, but instead of ships, allow your current mental and physical experience to pass by you, without a filter and without judgment. There's no need for you to react to whatever you think and feel—this is simply an observational experience.

Repeat this exercise a few times each week. With enough practice, you'll be able to foster a nonjudgmental mind-set toward anxious thoughts. By refraining from criticisms and negative judgments of your thoughts, you'll feel less of a need to worry and enjoy more tranquility.

Maladaptive Emotion Regulation Skills

As we mentioned earlier, "repetitive negative thinking" is a broad term used to describe worry and rumination. Worry is an abstract, verbal-linguistic process (talking to yourself, but in your head rather than out loud) oriented toward future threats, whereas rumination is a passive, persistent focus on the meaning and consequences of distressing feelings and situations (Borkovec, Alcaine, and Behar 2004; Nolen-Hoeksema, Wisco, and Lyubomirsky 2008).

Worry and rumination are common features of anxiety and occur in various contexts depending on the type of anxiety you have. For example, if you have an upcoming root canal, you might worry that the numbing medication won't work as well as you would like, you might worry about the procedure itself, or you might worry about your pain afterward. Rumination, on the other hand, is like getting together with friends to analyze a football game after a major loss for your team. It can also happen following anxiety-provoking situations, such as after a social interaction. Imagine accompanying your significant other to a wedding reception where you don't know any of the other guests. When your date disappears to talk to his or her friends, you escape to the bathroom or some other private area to avoid feeling insecure rather than make conversation with strangers. At home later that night, you might mentally review your perceived social failures during the reception. This form of mental review is fundamentally unproductive and unhelpful, because it likely would lead to undesirable emotional experiences or negative thoughts about yourself.

Worry and rumination may initially seem harmless, but both are involved in the generation of negative mood states.

Essentially, they needlessly breed negative thoughts and bring about anxious or even depressive mood states. Both also decrease your problem-solving abilities, sap your motivation, and make your friends and family less willing to lend you support. By increasing your awareness and mindfulness of triggers or cues that lead to worry and rumination, you may be able to reduce the consequences of repetitive negative thinking.

SUPPRESSION

Have you ever tried not to think about something? Perhaps you had a bad day at work and you wanted to avoid any thoughts or feelings associated with the day. Or maybe you witnessed a horrific accident that you don't ever want to think about again. If so, you may have utilized an emotion regulation strategy known as *suppression*. Suppression refers to a conscious attempt to stop thinking about a particular thought, situation, or event. Suppression has been shown to increase not only physiological reactivity (via the sympathetic nervous system, which controls the fight-or-flight response) but anxiety itself. Indeed, studies have shown that when subjects were specifically asked to suppress thoughts about anxiety-producing situations, not only did their thoughts not go away, but they reported feeling more anxious (Roemer and Borkovec 1994). Other research has shown that repeated suppression of emotionally evocative thoughts might make managing future anxiety-related thoughts more difficult (Wenzlaff and Wegner 2000). This is because long-term use of suppression as an emotion regulation strategy hinders your ability to learn how to appropriately manage and cope with your emotions over time.

AVOIDANCE

As we reviewed in chapter 3, not only can you choose to actively avoid certain objects or situations that elicit feelings of anxiety, you can choose to actively avoid emotions. Avoiding emotions is negatively reinforcing (see chapter 3) because it's associated with escaping from emotions you perceive as unpleasant or unbearable. Although avoidance provides some immediate relief when you feel anxious or worried, you deprive yourself of the chance to learn how to appropriately cope with the emotion and fully process it. If this happens often enough, you eventually lose the ability to properly process your emotions, solve problems, and cope well with negative thoughts and emotions.

᠅ ᠅ ᠅

The emotion regulation strategies presented in this chapter all represent ways of actively choosing to manage your emotional responses. The important thing to remember is to try to mindfully utilize more adaptive strategies, such as reappraisal, problem solving, acceptance, and decentering, as opposed to maladaptive strategies, such as suppression and avoidance. Also, know that old habits are hard to overcome and that effective emotion regulation is best accomplished with practice!

The mindfulness skills presented in this chapter are meant to be used in any situation, no matter how busy you are. Use them in combination with the specific emotion regulation strategies we illustrated to help you handle stressors more successfully. The key is to be flexible in your use of strategies. Using mindfulness will help you become more conscious of the present moment so that you can assess what emotions would be most helpful for you right now. Using the specific emotion regulation strategies in a flexible manner will help you gain mastery over your emotions. Together, these techniques can go a long way toward mindfully regulating your emotions.

chapter 6

Information Overload

The human brain is amazingly complex. It processes large amounts of information incredibly quickly. Although you are generally aware of your deliberate actions, many behaviors you perform are automatic and nearly imperceptible. Think about the last time you had a conversation with someone. Did you have to explicitly remember the laws of grammar in order to communicate? We doubt you planned which word would be the subject, which word would be the verb, which word would be the object, and so on. Your ability to speak with grammatical correctness comes naturally, because your brain is hardwired to compute and process information at a rapid speed. Likewise, certain other cognitive abilities—such as attention—rely on automatic, unconscious processing to coordinate large-scale behaviors.

We will explore how explicit and implicit attention processing interacts with anxiety, but first it may be useful to clarify exactly what we mean by the terms "explicit," "implicit," "conscious," and "unconscious."

Conscious vs. Unconscious Processing

The word "unconscious" has a long history in psychology, and it has referred to various phenomena at different times. The way we are using it here derives from cognitive science, which treats the brain as a computer and investigates what kinds of "computational machinery" are used to perform cognitive functions such as attention, vision, language, and decision making. It's important to distinguish this conceptualization of the unconscious from that posited by Sigmund Freud. The scientific literature has found little support for Freud's theory that the unconscious is the seat of inappropriate desires that are repressed from conscious awareness. Instead, the unconscious is used to refer to automatic cognitive processes that escape the notice of the person in whose mind they occur.

To illustrate this difference, we can take a look at a fascinating study that investigated implicit and explicit moral decision making (Hauser et al. 2007). In this study, people were presented with a variety of "trolley problems." (In psychology, a "trolley problem" usually entails the presentation of a moral dilemma in which a speeding train can take one of two tracks. One track will cause the train to collide with multiple people, killing them instantly. The other will cause the train to collide with just a single person. The participant in the study must decide on which track the train will travel. Is it best to do nothing and let fate take its course, killing a number of people, or is it best to divert the train and purposely kill one person in favor of saving several? There are many variations on this basic idea, but overall it's used to derive basic moral decision-making rules to which most people adhere.) In this particular experiment, participants were asked to (a) decide whether the train would run over a single person or a group of five people and (b) justify their decision. The results of the study suggested that people adopted implicit decision-making principles to guide their choice but were unable to provide an explicit justification that corresponded to this principle.

In one variation of the "trolley problem," participants learned that the train would run over a group of five individuals who were trapped on the track. However, on a bridge directly above the train track was a heavyset man whose weight would be sufficient to stop the train if participants shoved him off the bridge. The participants were then asked whether it would be permissible to push this man off the bridge and thereby kill him in the service of saving the lives of five other people. Most participants declared that it wouldn't be permissible, and the pattern of results indicated that these participants were appealing to an implicit principle: the *proximity principle*. This principle holds that a person is less likely to save a larger number of people by harming a smaller number of people if he or she must get physically close to them to do so. Because saving the lives of the five people would require participants to physically push the heavyset man off the bridge, they were less inclined to consider such an action permissible, even though it would save lives. Most of the participants, however, didn't give an explicit justification that aligned with the proximity principle. It seemed as if their conscious thoughts were at odds with their unconscious cognitive processes.

So, you might wonder, how does all of this relate to anxiety? This is an excellent question that has received a great amount of attention in the scientific literature. Empirical evidence has suggested that unconscious attentional process underlie emotions, which isn't too hard to imagine. If there were a lion racing after you, your anxiety would immediately draw your attention to this threatening beast. You wouldn't need to deliberate over whether you should pay attention to the lion; it would automatically happen. If anxiety didn't focus people's attention in this way, we wouldn't have survived as a species. In some instances, however, people's attentional processes can become biased. They may attend to negative stimuli too frequently or for too long, which can result in unnecessary fear or distress. In the following sections, we will describe how biased attention plays a role in anxiety and what we can do about it. But first, it might be helpful to examine how explicit and implicit processes play a role in emotion regulation.

Explicit vs. Implicit Emotion Regulation

Remember the last time you were in a rush to get to work or to an appointment? If luck wasn't on your side, perhaps due to heavy traffic or your alarm clock not going off, you might have felt nervous or angry. In what way did you respond to your emotions, and how did you know what to do? Did you purposefully try to manage your emotions, or was it an automatic reaction? In this section, we will review the difference between actively (on purpose) regulating your emotions and more automatic (unconscious) responses.

A good deal of this book has so far focused on the use of *explicit*, or effortful, emotion regulation strategies for managing your anxiety. In this context, the term "explicit" refers to processes that underlie your efforts to actively respond to and modify your emotional experience. These include making a conscious and deliberate effort to regulate your emotions, awareness and insight into the strategies you use, and the ability to monitor and flexibly modify strategies as a situation demands (Gyurak, Gross, and Etkin 2011). These explicit processes work together so that you can flexibly use one or more strategies to purposefully influence your responses to your emotions.

Along the same continuum, you also use *implicit*, or automatic and unconscious, processes that help you regulate your emotions. Implicit processes operate largely outside of your awareness and without deliberation or mindful attention (similar to your breathing or the beating of your heart). Implicit emotion regulation processes also underlie many maladaptive emotion regulation strategies. For example, have you ever thought it might be relaxing to have a cold drink after a long day at work or to eat a pint of your favorite ice cream to cheer yourself up when you were feeling down? If so, even though you may have actively chosen to engage in that specific behavior, it probably resulted from a well-established and instinctive habit that you developed over time to cope with certain emotions.

Practice   Take a moment to consider some of your explicit and implicit emotion regulation responses, and record them on a piece of paper for later use. Since these can be hard to identify, especially implicit strategies, try to think of responses to emotional experiences that you've had during the past few days. For example, if you had a big presentation coming up at work that made you feel quite anxious, an explicit response to this emotion would have been to call in sick the day before to avoid the experience altogether. An implicit response might have been a tendency to avoid eye contact with audience members while giving the presentation because it temporarily made your distress less intense.

How Cognitive Biases Darken Your Emotional Experiences

Your cognitions, or your thoughts, are closely linked to your emotions. Indeed, theories on the relationship between thoughts and emotions suggest that the way you think about a particular situation determines not only whether you experience an emotion but also the type of emotion you experience. Cognitions, therefore, are the principal pathways through which you can both understand and regulate your emotional experiences.

For example, if you tend to be nervous about social interactions, you may be prone to think that you are not socially skilled. As a consequence, you may feel lonely due to your reluctance to attend social gatherings. Each time you have a negative thought about your social abilities, it will likely trigger a range of emotional experiences, including anxiety about future social interactions and possibly sadness about your loneliness. If you wanted to better regulate your emotions so that you felt more confident in social situations, you would likely benefit from reappraising your initial thought.

One of the more common questions we receive from people who have anxiety is *why* they experience negative or irrational thoughts. Although there's not a single straightforward answer, especially because the content of each individual's thoughts is highly variable, it's generally accepted that negative and irrational thoughts often arise from the ways in which people relate to and interpret their environment. Ordinarily, this shouldn't be a problem. Sometimes, however, the volume of information that individuals, especially anxious individuals, have to make sense of and process is too much to handle. Although the human brain is remarkably well equipped to process a great deal of incoming information, it has its limits. To overcome these limits, people use *heuristics*, or mental shortcuts or rules, to deal with both simple and complex or ambiguous stimuli. These heuristics essentially are informal and intuitive algorithms, or "rules of thumb," that our brains use for rapid problem solving and general reasoning.

Heuristics can be incredibly adaptive and helpful. There are heuristics that help you avoid dangerous animals, heuristics that help you solve problems, heuristics that help you know when to trust people, and heuristics that help you make snap judgments. The downside is that heuristics are prone to error. For example, one of the more well-known heuristics, the *availability heuristic*, occurs when you make judgments about the probability of something happening based on how easily examples come to mind. In one study published in 1974, two psychological scientists, Amos Tversky and Daniel Kahneman, asked participants to decide whether more words in the English language began with the letter K (such as "kite," "kabob," and "kick") or whether more words had the letter K in the third position (such as "cake," "joke," and "hike"). Despite the fact that there are twice as many English words with K in the third position than in the first, most participants reported the opposite because it was easier for them to recall words that began with K.

Heuristics can also be problematic for your anxious emotions. For example, if you have a fear of rats, you may have developed a rule that all furry creatures that look and act like rats should be treated as threats. Therefore, when you encounter any rodent (a mouse, a gopher, a chipmunk, and so on), you perceive it as threatening and react in an anxious way. Similarly, if you have a fear of germs, you might believe that all public surfaces—such as door handles, shopping carts, and bathroom sink counters—are dangerous and should be avoided. Your thoughts related to encountering these feared surfaces will invariably lead you to feel anxiety.

Heuristics, over time, tend to lead to *cognitive bias,* or a type of error in thinking caused by simplified information-processing strategies. Some psychologists call cognitive biases "thought habits." Thought habits arise as automatic, characteristic ways of thinking about the world and your relation to it. For example, people are generally biased in favor of people who hold views that are similar to their own and who agree with them. It's why you might tend to have friends who are similarly minded to you, why you like certain television news programs over others, or even why you spend time reading certain websites. Another example of a bias occurs after you buy a new car or hear a catchy new song. Unexpectedly, you see that same model of car or hear that same song everywhere, because it's suddenly more relevant to you. Yet another example of a common bias is that people, on average, tend to pay more attention to bad news than to good news. This is because people place a higher importance on negative news—after all, it's more adaptive to know about the dangers around us than it is to know about the works of a humanitarian. These cognitive biases and many more are caused by a number of factors, including memories, attention, learning, and social pressures.

Individuals with anxiety disorders and those who are more prone to experience anxiety tend to be especially disposed to both attention and interpretation cognitive biases (Beard 2011). *Attention bias* refers to the tendency of anxious people to pay more attention to threatening stimuli, including interoceptive awareness (see chapter 2), to guard against threat. This notion has been well studied using simple computer-measured tasks, such as the dot-probe paradigm. During the dot-probe task, individuals are simultaneously shown (on a computer screen) a pair of words, one neutral (such as "bicycle") and one threatening (such as "cancer"). The words are displayed for only a very short time, less than a thousandth of a second. After the words disappear, a dot appears where one of the words was, and the participants' task is to locate the dot as quickly as possible. Anxious participants are typically quicker to locate the dot when it appears where the threatening word was compared with where the neutral word was, indicating that they are more vigilant against threatening words. Participants without anxiety, however, don't share this tendency. Examination of such studies reveals that not only is attention bias related to anxiety, attention bias may increase the likelihood that people will develop problematic or disordered anxiety.

Interpretation bias refers to anxious people's tendency not only to focus on negative events and emotions but also to interpret ambiguous stimuli in a negative or calamitous manner. Memory may play an important role in interpretation bias, such that anxious individuals tend to more frequently recall negative events while dismissing or forgetting positive events. For example, if you have a fear of dogs and you encounter an off-leash dog while walking in a park, you may be more prone to remember all of your past negative (scary) encounters with dogs than to remember your past positive encounters. Similar to research on attention biases, research on interpretation biases reveals a strong connection to problematic anxiety.

If you struggle with anxiety, learning to modify your cognitive biases may help you change your responses to emotion-eliciting events and, therefore, better regulate your emotions. You can learn to monitor, catch, and modify your thought habits when they occur; not only does modifying your biases help you better interpret your day-to-day experiences, the changes in your interpretations of your environment may improve your memory by giving you more data to work with. One way to modify your cognitive biases is through a strategy known as *attentional deployment*, which we will examine below. We will discuss other strategies, such as cognitive bias modification, in later chapters.

How Mindfulness and Attentional Training Can Reduce Threatening Emotions

Attention, much like a microscope, helps you selectively bring into focus and magnify various aspects of your world. As previously mentioned in this book, attention involves both cognition and behavior, which work together to allow you to filter essential information from the superfluous. When your attention becomes overfocused on detecting threats, increasing your use of attentional processes can help you effectively and more appropriately shape your emotional experiences.

Attention helps you remain alert, focused, and better able to manage the mental processes involved in planning, problem solving, organizing, and making important decisions. As an emotion regulation strategy, attention, or more specifically *attentional deployment*, influences how you respond to emotions by redirecting your attention within a given situation (Gross and Thompson 2007). In this sense, attentional deployment can be either a strategy in itself or used as a component of other strategies, such as reappraisal or problem solving.

Attentional deployment is considered to be a foundational aspect of mindfulness practice. It has been shown to improve not only attention skills in general but also the use of both implicit and explicit emotion regulation processes. It does this in two key ways. First, it helps you distract yourself from emotional situations by shifting your attention or by shifting your focus. For example, if you are watching a scary scene of a movie, you might cover your eyes or look away to shift your attention; however, if you want to altogether shift your focus, you might try to think of something unrelated to the movie, such as a fun family vacation. Second, it's useful for focused concentration, or devoting your full attention to a particular activity. Essentially, you choose exactly what to focus on so that you can purposefully regulate your emotions. Hopefully these two components of attentional deployment sound familiar, given their strong role in cultivating a more mindful approach to regulating your emotions.

Outsmarting Anxiety Skill #5:
Reduce conscious and unconscious threats
to your emotional well-being.

Suggested Practices

Before you begin the following practices, remember the guidelines we provided in chapter 2. It's important that you be consistent and patient. Practice daily, and be forgiving with yourself if you make a mistake!

One thing about attention is that it's often directed inward when you feel anxious. In other words, whenever you feel anxious you are often paying attention to your thoughts, feelings, and bodily sensations rather than paying attention to what's going on around you. Moreover, this internal focus makes it very easy to become fixated on perceived threats, which is why your attentional processes can become biased over time. A technique called "attention training," developed by Adrian Wells (2011), can help with this problem by teaching you how to cultivate greater control over your attention.

Exercise 6.1: **Attention Training**   Before you begin, put yourself in an environment in which there are multiple continuous sounds. For example, try entering a room where you can hear an air conditioner running and a clock ticking. The more sounds there are, the more benefit you can gain from performing this exercise.

1. Try to identify a single sound—for example, the hum of the air conditioner—and focus on it exclusively. If you notice a sound from another source, direct your attention back to the one you are focusing on. Really try to become deeply immersed in this one sound. After you feel you have been able to do this continuously for about one minute, transition to another sound—for example, the ticking of the clock. Focus your attention on it until you are aware of only this particular sound. Again, continue this for about one minute. After you have been able to focus on each sound exclusively, alternate your attention between these two sound sources. Whenever you focus on one, attend to it at the exclusion of the other. Spend about five minutes total on this step.

2. This step is very similar to the first step, with one important difference. Instead of slowly alternating between sounds, this time you will *quickly* alternate. Try spending ten seconds on each sound. You should still try to focus all of your attention on just one sound, even if only for a short time. Should your attention wane, redirect your focus to the appropriate sound. Spend about five minutes on this step too.

3. Now, notice two sounds *at the same time*. For example, notice the ticking of the clock and the hum of the air conditioner simultaneously. Then add a third sound (such as the sound of traffic outside your house, the wind through the trees, or the conversation of someone adjacent to you). Keep adding sounds. Your goal is to divide your attention among as many sounds as you can find in your immediate surroundings. This will teach you to expand your attention and take in the whole sum of your perceptual experience. Try to practice this for one minute.

To summarize, this attention training technique entails five minutes of undivided attention with slow alternations, five minutes of undivided attention with quick alternations, and one minute of divided attention. Practice it once or twice a day; use it to complement the other mindfulness techniques in this book. This will allow you to achieve greater mastery over your attention, making it less likely that you will engage in prolonged worry cycles and be biased to assume the worst about a situation.

Exercise 6.2: **Mantra Meditation** We have already described using your breath as an object on which you may focus your attention. Many meditators complement this technique with using a mantra to facilitate meditation. This approach entails the selection of a word, sound, or nonsense syllable that you will repeat in synchrony with your breath. A very popular choice is "Om," but if that seems too clichéd or feels uncomfortable, feel free to use a different word, sound, or nonsense syllable. We will give you two ways to practice mantra meditation.

The Inhale-Exhale Practice

Try to find a quiet place without distractions, and start the non-judgmental breath meditation you learned in chapter 4. This time, you will be adding your mantra on top of your breath when you inhale and exhale. Let us say that you decided upon "Om" as your mantra. You would slowly say "Om" when you take a deep breath in and when you exhale. So, it would look like this:

Breathe in: "Ommmmmmmm."
Breathe out: "Ommmmmmmm."

Breathe in: "Ommmmmmmm."
Breathe out: "Ommmmmmmm."

Your main goal is to focus all of your attention on your mantra, whatever it may be. As with other mindfulness practices you have learned in this book, your observation and focus as you meditate should be of a nonjudgmental and nonreactive nature. Any time a distressing thought intrudes upon your mind, you need not respond with threatening interpretations. Instead, merely note the thought and then redirect your attention, which is the healthy opposite of having a cognitive bias. Remember how cognitive biases force your attention to the most negative aspects of a situation or thought? This encourages worrying and rumination. Practicing nonjudgmental meditation will train your mind to let go of cognitive biases and replace them with a less reactive form of attention.

The Exhale Practice

Instead of saying "Om" when you inhale and exhale, try saying it only when you exhale; while inhaling, direct your attention to your breath. As in the attention training exercise, by alternating your attention to different stimuli, you are strengthening your ability to focus. This style of mantra meditation would look like this:

Breathe in: silence... Breathe out: "Ommmmmmmm."

Breathe in: silence... Breathe out: "Ommmmmmmm."

The next time you try practicing the nonjudgmental breath exercises in chapter 4, try out these two mantra meditation exercises. Try to spend five minutes with each style. If you practice this in concert with the attention training exercise, then you will be well on your way to achieving mastery over your concentration, making it less susceptible to cognitive biases and unhelpful emotion regulation strategies.

❁ ❁ ❁

In this chapter, we introduced the concept of unconscious cognitive biases and their role in anxiety. The idea behind cognitive biases hinges on the distinction between conscious and unconscious processes, or, put another way, implicit and explicit attention.

There are many mental acts of which you are explicitly aware and can visualize. When it comes to anxiety, you may be able to imagine a humiliating speech or the worst-case scenario of some future event. Many aspects of anxiety, however, remain unnoticed, occurring behind the scenes and away from your conscious awareness. Individuals who experience high levels of anxiety tend to develop cognitive biases that disproportionately focus their attention on threatening objects and thoughts. Such biases may make it more likely that you would notice a look of dissatisfaction in another person or even mistakenly interpret a neutral facial expression as angry! To help you counteract this, in this chapter we introduced two techniques that target attentional control, building on the mindfulness techniques you have learned so far. By exercising this important mental muscle, you will be in a better position to use your attention in a nonjudgmental, nonreactive manner that will decrease the influence of your cognitive biases.

chapter 7

Feeling Bad Is Actually Good

Have you ever found yourself struggling to accept a gift? Maybe someone gave you a gift that was incredibly disappointing or cringe-worthy and you had to fake a smile. For instance, what if your wife bought you a nose-hair trimmer for your birthday or your husband bought tickets to see *his* favorite band in concert for your anniversary? What if your mother-in-law gave you a *Cookbook for Beginners* or your holiday bonus was a cheap keychain with the company logo on it?

Despite the internal struggle people may have to graciously accept an inconsiderate gift, most everyone probably finds a way to feign excitement and express gratitude (perhaps all the while scheming how to exchange or repurpose what they've gotten). Fortunately, most people receive many more thoughtful and exciting gifts in their lifetime than they do tactless or insensitive gifts. It turns out that emotions are a lot like gifts. Oftentimes, you probably enjoy and welcome your emotional experiences, much like thoughtful gifts. Nonetheless, certain emotional experiences might feel like a significant threat to your well-being (like the nose-hair trimmer or the *Beginners* book) and lead you to attempt to deny your emotional experience. In this chapter, we will explain why sometimes feeling bad is necessary to feeling good.

Fostering Emotional Acceptance with Mindfulness

Learning to skillfully and successfully regulate your emotions is a healthy endeavor not only because it will help you manage your everyday experiences but also because it will improve your overall well-being. Living a meaningful and authentic life implies openness to and acceptance of a full array of emotional experiences, including pleasant and unpleasant emotions. Accepting emotions entails an unrestricted openness to—meaning you don't try to control, avoid, or change—both your emotions *and* the processes that accompany them (that is, thoughts and bodily sensations). It also requires a persistent level of engagement with your emotions, regardless of their *valence*, or their inherent attractiveness or aversiveness (happiness, for example, has a positive valence because it has an attractive quality, whereas anger has a negative valence because it's thought to have an aversive quality). Indeed, research in this area supports the notion that accepting emotions is associated with long-term psychological health (see, for example, Plumb, Orsillo, and Luterek 2004) and with decreased anxiety and depression (see, for example, Tull et al. 2004; Campbell-Sills et al. 2006; Hofmann et al. 2009). Thus, the goal of this chapter is to encourage you to work toward accepting your emotions to better manage your anxiety. It's best to think of acceptance on a continuum rather than categorically (that is, either accepting or not accepting your emotion). Following are strategies, or ways of thinking about your emotions, to help you nurture an attitude of acceptance and to reduce your emotional distress.

Emotions are more than feelings. Emotions, at least from a Western cultural perspective, are often thought to be most valuable when they are subjectively pleasant. Indeed, if you were to informally poll your family, friends, and work colleagues, you would likely find that most people generally want to feel good. More specifically, they purposefully try to cultivate experiences that generate positive emotions (joy, contentment, love, and so on) and avoid unpleasant experiences that produce negative emotions (worry, anger, shame, and so on) (see, for example, Larsen 2000). However, emotions are more than mere feelings to be enjoyed or tolerated. Instead, emotions are thought to cohere and interact to serve some function or purpose, whether it's to survive, thrive, communicate, or validate internal experiences. Everyday life is fairly complex, and rarely, if ever, do people experience a single emotion in isolation. People can strive for pleasant experiences, but pleasant experiences are never guaranteed. A critical skill in learning to regulate emotions is learning to accept both the good and the bad.

Although the view that emotions have a hedonistic basis is generally true, it tends to oversimplify the complexity of the human emotional experience. Feelings are only one component of emotions. Emotions have the following functions:

- To help you construe or interpret what's happening in your environment

- To help you behave or act in a way that fits with your internal motivations and external environment

- To help you express your subjective experiences to others

To illustrate these three components, imagine that while on a hike with friends, you encounter a ferocious-looking cougar and her three kittens. Even though you know it's rare for a cougar to attack a human, you feel a rush of fear and panic (*feeling*). Your emotional reaction helps you assess your level of danger (*construal or appraisal*) and how to act (*behavior*) by leading you to slowly back away. Your friends, who haven't yet seen the cougar, notice you look scared and that you are acting uncharacteristically odd (*expression of emotion*). Your demeanor, body language, and behavior all serve as a way of informing others, through your emotion, of the potential danger.

Practice Identify a situation or activity from the past week and try to label each of the following:

- Your emotion

- Your cognitive construal or appraisal of the situation

- What action you took or how you behaved

- The emotion (or emotions) that you expressed to others

Now, take a moment to repeat this exercise by using an emotion with a different valence from the first scenario. For example, if your emotion in the first scenario was a positive emotion, repeat the exercise by using a situation or activity from the past week that entailed a negative emotion. Use this exercise to repeatedly (two to three times per week) focus on anxious emotions so that you can better understand their *function*.

The multicomponent theory of emotions (more simply: a theory that states emotions have many components) allows researchers (and you!) to explore the idea that emotions are driven, at least in part, by their usefulness for achieving particular goals. In this sense, both positive and negative emotions have potential to be, on average, equally beneficial to a person who has a particular goal in mind. The emotion itself, of course, will vary depending on the situation, on the circumstances, and on the nature of the goal. Thus, you may choose to regulate positive *or* negative emotions to feel a certain way for a particular purpose. For example, if while walking through a public park you notice a crowd of people who appear to be decidedly entertained by a group of street performers, you might experience positive emotions, such as amusement, interest, and even joy. These emotions might prompt you to join the crowd and engage with the performance to build on your already positive state. Alternatively, the benefits of negative emotions may be seen in the context of anxiety. Imagine that you had a serious argument with a romantic partner or good friend. Your anxiety, although unpleasant, might motivate you to try to address the argument and/or repair the relationship.

Practice   Identify two positive and two negative emotions that you have experienced in the past month. Intense emotions, or emotions that you felt strongly, might be easier to analyze. For each emotion, label:

- The situation or context in which the emotion occurred

- The circumstances that led up to the emotion

- The goal you were trying to achieve

Positive emotions are good to a point. If you have ever felt besieged by your emotions, particularly negative ones, such as anxiety and fear, you may have found yourself wishing for endless days of blissful contentment stemming from positive emotional experiences. After all, who wouldn't want to feel happy, content, and satisfied all the time?

It turns out, rather surprisingly, that psychologically healthy people know that when it comes to positive emotions, more is not necessarily better, *and* positive emotions aren't always preferable to negative ones (Haybron 2014). Practically, positive emotions are good, but only to a point. In fact, having an overabundance of positive emotion too often is similar to eating cake for every meal or repeatedly playing your new favorite song. At first, it feels great to overindulge, but eventually, you find that too much of a good thing can have unintended consequences (like that sick feeling you get from eating too much sugar or eventually loathing that new song). Cultivating too much positive emotion, or only positive emotion, can also be problematic because not all emotions are suited to every context or situation. Imagine, for example, meeting someone who is cheerful at a funeral or seeing a friend or colleague joyfully bully someone.

Practice   Identify two or three positive emotion-enhancing strategies that you tend to overuse, even if only slightly, to help regulate your mood. For example, when nervous, perhaps you think of positive memories or watch a favorite movie or listen to your favorite album. Some people rely on friends or family to help them manage their mood, whereas others turn to tension-relieving hobbies or vices such as alcohol and/or drugs. Once you have identified a list of emotion-enhancing strategies, keep track of how often you use them throughout the following week (or for a month, if you want a real challenge). While so doing, analyze these emotions using the previous practice.

An imbalance between positive and negative emotion can also have unintended effects in terms of the authenticity of your emotional responses. *Authentic emotional responses* are emotions that reflect your personal values and how you feel based on the circumstances of your life (Haybron 2014). These emotions are typically characterized by sincerity or genuineness and spontaneity. Children, for example, have a great ability to authentically express their emotions; they rarely attempt to protect or shield themselves or others from their emotional experiences.

Cultivating authentic emotional experiences requires learning to tolerate emotions *regardless of their valence.* This entails openness to your emotional experiences irrespective of how they make you feel and allowing them to develop naturally without trying to avoid or escape the reality of your current situation. It also requires mindful awareness of your long-term goals (to reduce your anxiety and increase your well-being) rather than focusing on short-term goals (such as to alleviate your present-moment suffering). Striving for authenticity in your emotional responses facilitates learning how to appropriately cope with your emotions as well as validates and increases your chance of more fully accepting your emotional experiences. Although you may be inclined to turn to positive emotion to assuage your anxiety, locating the proper balance between positive and negative emotions to accept your anxious emotions (or any emotions!) is an important goal.

Practice   Over the next month, practice being emotionally authentic at least once a week. Your goal is to be true or virtuous in your emotional response to your life's circumstances. This might mean not trying to stifle your response, or it might mean answering a question honestly—for example, when someone asks, "How are you doing?" you respond with an honest answer rather than an automatic "fine," "okay," or "well." Remember, being authentic in your emotions is a collection of choices, and it's based on a continuum; it's not that you either are or are not authentic but that you strive for authenticity.

Note: Be cautious about how, where, and with whom you do this. Be smart about when to practice authenticity and when not to. It may be wise, at first, to choose to be authentic only when by yourself. If something makes you happy and you feel like laughing, then laugh. Or dance, or sing, or cry, or choose simply to be you.

The Positive Side of Negative Emotions

Epicurus, an ancient Greek philosopher, spent a large part of his life examining what makes people happy. He believed that above all else, people desire happiness and that all other desires are a means of achieving happiness. He further believed that wisdom gained through life experience would inform people about which pleasures are truly pleasurable *and*, importantly, which pains are necessary to produce pleasure—in other words, why feeling good is good and why feeling bad is also good.

According to his philosophy, activities in life are generally pursued according to their value, including whether they have *intrinsic* or *instrumental value*. Activities characterized by intrinsic value are those that are naturally pleasurable (for example, a person who enjoys exercise might walk to the store), whereas instrumental activities are motivated by their future intrinsic value, or their long-term reward (for example, a person who values health might walk to the store because it fulfills a long-term goal of being healthy, even if it's not an enjoyable activity). If this concept still isn't clear, imagine writing a book! During the actual writing process, there may be very little intrinsic value but a good deal of instrumental value. Emotions, and the ways in which people regulate them, can be viewed from this same perspective, but with one caveat: positive emotions naturally have both intrinsic and instrumental value, but negative emotions typically only have instrumental value. Indeed, it's rare for people to increase their negative emotions based on any immediate intrinsic (pleasurable) value.

Practice   Label the following activities in terms of their intrinsic or instrumental emotional properties and explain *why*. For example, if you were given the example of *cleaning your bedroom,* you might label it as *instrumental* because it has long-term value (you value a clean room, find it more peaceful, will be less stressed about the messes, and so on).

- Dieting

- Shopping for shoes

- Kayaking for sport

- Smoking to calm your nerves

- Studying for a test

- Installing solar panels

Next, create a list of five to ten activities you do each week and practice labeling them in terms of their intrinsic or instrumental emotional properties.

The value of negative emotions can be best understood in the context of what they motivate you to do (their instrumental value), rather than simply how they make you feel. Remember, emotions are more than a feeling. If you were to simply tolerate the feeling of a particular negative emotion (or group of emotions) for the mere sake of doing so, it would be uncomfortable at best and torturous at worst. There would be no intrinsic value. However, if you took time to examine the motivating factor of the emotion, you could usually overcome the negative and unpleasant feeling by engaging in some purposeful or goal-directed activity.

To illustrate, let's examine the emotional experience of dissatisfaction. If you have ever felt dissatisfied with how much your anxiety interferes with your life, you are probably well aware that the feeling itself can lead to a good deal of discomfort, distress, and displeasure. For that reason, few people willingly connect with the emotion of anxiety without trying to control, avoid, or change it. Nonetheless, dissatisfaction is what drives achievement in your life; this emotion, then, if fully understood and accepted, might prompt you to work toward meaningfully reducing your anxiety by following the tips outlined in this book.

Other theories on the utility of negative emotions are rooted in evolutionary psychology. Emotions are thought to have evolved as a way of maximizing our ancestors' survival. Anxiety certainly accords well with these theories.

Specifically, fear-based (that is, fight-or-flight) and anxiety-based (that is, worry and avoidance) reactions help people survive and avoid injury (Perkins and Corr 2014). These emotional reactions certainly are instrumental in nature; without either emotion, the human population might be very different (for one thing, there would be far fewer of us!). Sadness is yet another example of a negative emotion that has adaptive properties (Forgas 2014b). Specifically, it has been shown that sadness can activate cognitive and behavioral strategies that are well suited to managing the requirements of a demanding emotional situation (Frijda 1986). To review, negative emotions encompass a wide array of useful functions, including (a) motivating individual behavior, (b) guiding thoughts, attention, and memory, (c) communicating information to yourself and others, and (d) prompting additional useful emotional experiences.

Practice   Take a moment to consider how your anxiety has both motivating and adaptive properties and contrast these with how you actually respond to your emotions in real life. For example, perhaps you characteristically avoid that which makes you anxious, but in reality, your emotion is prompting you to confront and overcome your fear.

Mindfully Accepting Emotions

Mindfulness has been shown to confer a number of benefits for successful regulation of emotions, including fostering acceptance of both positive and negative emotions. Research on mindfulness has consistently shown that higher *dispositional mindfulness*, or one's awareness and attention on a day-to-day basis (in contrast to a moment-to-moment basis or mindfulness that is more trait-like), helps buffer the negative effects of negative emotions (see, for example, Arch and Craske 2010; Hill and Updegraff 2012). Specifically, dispositional mindfulness reduces the tendency to use suppression as an emotion management strategy by fostering a greater willingness to engage with emotionally negative thoughts. Mindfulness also promotes sustained contact with aversive emotions and increases your capacity to nonjudgmentally accept your emotional experience(s). In turn, this leads to more effective moment-to-moment processing of emotions and decreased use of maladaptive regulation processes, such as rumination, worry, and avoidance.

Mindfulness has also been shown to increase tolerance of negative emotions. In one study, participants were shown pictures containing negative (objectionable and explicit) content. Participants who were instructed to breathe mindfully while viewing the pictures ultimately reported experiencing less negative emotion and were more willing to view additional content (Arch and Craske 2006). Another study found that emotion regulation statistically accounted for the relationship between mindfulness and psychological distress. This means that emotion regulation helps explain why those with higher levels of mindfulness have lower levels of psychological distress (from anxiety, depression, and other disorders; Coffey and Hartmann 2008). Together, these studies suggest that greater tolerance of negative emotions as a result of mindfulness may facilitate reduced cognitive and emotional reactivity and increased ability to work through negative emotions (Erisman and Roemer 2010).

Internal vs. External Anxiety Stimuli

You are likely well aware that external stimuli, or situations or objects in your environment, can lead to anxiety. We have covered many examples in this book thus far, but as a very brief refresher, almost anything in the environment, including other people, animals, natural disasters, germs, and even everyday objects, can make people feel anxious. Sometimes anxiety is adaptive and helps you avoid harm, and sometimes it amounts to nothing more than a false alarm. Anxiety can also arise from *internal experiences*: thoughts, emotions, and bodily sensations. When people experience anxiety, especially these false alarms, they tend to negatively judge themselves for thinking and feeling (both emotionally and physically) the way they do. What this tells us is that the problem isn't anxiety itself; instead, it's the problematic way you respond to your internal experiences. This way of responding not only exacerbates your anxiety but also allows it to persist over the long term. Further, it leads to avoidance of situations or experiences that you associate (through conditioning) with your anxiety. Avoidance strategies usually include attempts to change the intensity and/or frequency of your internal experiences through suppression or outright behavioral avoidance. For example, if you are irrationally worried about something, you might try to avoid thinking about your worry by distracting yourself, physically removing yourself from the situation, or actively trying to suppress the content from your mind.

Outsmarting Anxiety Skill #6:
Accept your emotions.

Suggested Practices

Mindfulness is useful for counteracting the adverse effects of anxiety resulting from both external and internal stimuli. Specifically, it facilitates an opportunity to expose yourself to internal experiences without judgment or reactivity. By increasing attention to your thoughts, emotions, and bodily sensations without trying to change, dismiss, or suppress them, you will reduce your reactivity to and increase your acceptance of your emotions. Do the mindfulness practices that follow at least once a week, if not once a day. It's not realistic to expect changes after one or two practices. Remember, acceptance is an incremental striving; it may be easier on some days compared with others or even for some emotions compared with others.

The following practices build on one another, and it's best to do them in order. Once you feel comfortable with each practice, move on to the next one *without abandoning the previous one*. It's preferable to do these practices while in a calm and safe state of mind rather than during times of extreme stress, emotional or otherwise. Always prioritize your own psychological safety and health. You may want to record yourself reading each of these practices aloud. This will enable you to experience a relatively distraction-free mindfulness practice. This also has the added benefit of being usable on a portable device, such as your smartphone. Finally, allow yourself room to grow with each practice, and remember that perfection isn't the goal.

Exercise 7.1: **Turn Toward the Emotion**   Once you become aware of a feeling, take a moment to pause and simply acknowledge that you are feeling an emotion. Try not to label or judge the emotion, but simply notice its presence. As you connect more strongly with the emotion, observe without judgment your experience (remember the puppy analogy from chapter 2). Try not to inhibit, avoid, suppress, or overcome the emotion. If you notice yourself turning away from the emotion, try to bring your awareness back to the emotion. Simply try to cultivate an open attitude toward the emotion. Do this at least three times a week, for three minutes.

Exercise 7.2: **Identify the Emotion**   Once you become aware of a feeling, take a moment to pause and simply acknowledge that you are feeling an emotion. After ten to fifteen seconds, label the emotion as specifically as possible.

Here is a list to help you (available for download at the website for this book):

Angry	Loathsome	Creative
Fearful	Astonished	Lonely
Happy	Hostile	Contemptuous
Sad	Confused	Confused
Disgusted	Cheerful	Critical
Surprised	Ashamed	Helpless
Hurt	Detestable	Fascinated
Anxious	Startled	Bored
Excited	Hateful	Offended
Guilty	Terrified	Amazed

Selfish	Jealous	Annoyed
Submissive	Discouraged	Overwhelmed
Stimulated	Optimistic	Serene
Tired	Apathetic	Devastated
Repulsed	Dread	Reviled
Excited	Disillusioned	Eager
Distant	Irritated	Enraged
Insecure	Inadequate	Scared
Amused	Elated	Joyful
Depressed	Pensive	Sorrowful
Sickened	Disapproving	Disapproving
Dismayed	Awed	Flabbergasted
Frustrated	Skeptical	Bitter
Bewildered	Embarrassed	Appalled
Playful	Exuberant	Amazed
Remorseful	Mournful	Despairing
Revolted	Hesitant	Repugnant
Shocked	Perplexed	Bewildered

(You can also search the Internet for "emotion chart," "list of emotions," or "emotion faces." Many websites and images contain comprehensive lists of emotions. Use these, as appropriate or applicable, to label your emotion.) Continue to sit with the emotion and try not to judge it, but simply notice its presence. Try not to inhibit, avoid, suppress, or overcome the emotion. If you notice yourself

Don't Let Anxiety Run Your Life

turning away from your emotion, try to bring your awareness back to the emotion. Simply try to cultivate an open attitude toward the emotion. Do this at least three times a week, for five minutes.

Exercise 7.3: **Accept the Emotion**   Once you become aware of a feeling, take a moment to pause and simply acknowledge that you are feeling an emotion. After ten to fifteen seconds, label the emotion as specifically as possible. Continue to sit with the emotion, and try not to judge it but simply notice its presence. Now, focus on the emotion, as well as any thoughts you have about the emotion. Resist the urge to react, inhibit, avoid, suppress, or overcome the emotion. If you notice yourself turning away from the emotion, try to bring your awareness back to the emotion, as well as your thoughts about the emotion. Simply try to cultivate an attitude of acceptance toward the emotion. Do this at least two times a week, for ten minutes.

Exercise 7.4: **Fully Accept the Emotion**   Once you become aware of a feeling, take a moment to pause and simply acknowledge that you are feeling an emotion. After ten to fifteen seconds, label the emotion as specifically as possible. Continue to sit with the emotion, and try not to judge it but simply notice its presence. Now, focus on the emotion, any thoughts you have about the emotion, and any bodily sensations you have in response to the emotion. Resist the urge to react, inhibit, avoid, suppress, or overcome the emotion. If you notice yourself turning away from the emotion, try to bring your awareness back to the emotion, as well as your thoughts about the emotion. Simply try to cultivate an attitude of acceptance toward the emotion. Do this at least twice a week, for ten minutes.

Repeat exercises 7.1–7.4 by connecting to both pleasant and unpleasant emotions (separately, not simultaneously).

chapter 8

Unhelpful Habits

Anxiety can prove difficult to overcome, in part because it's deep-seated and ingrained. It's not as if you have complete control over when you feel nervous. Cues from your surrounding environment can prompt you to turn on your internal alarm clock. Being driven to pay attention to certain kinds of information leads you to form interpretations that are hard to dispute. Think about entering a scary social situation: What's the first thing you notice? Well, often it's not good. An innocuous environment can appear to be a threatening arena of glares, stares, and judgment. Taking what you learned in chapter 6, we will explore additional ways to conquer the cognitive and attentional biases that darken your experiences.

Attention and Confronting Your Fears

You have likely heard the phrase "seeing things through rose-colored glasses." Individuals suffering from anxiety exhibit a tendency to see things through dark-colored glasses. In other words, their world is fraught with threats and danger. Seemingly neutral objects can transform into instruments of harm (for example, a piece of rope is seen as a snake). These cognitive biases can make confronting your fears much more daunting than it need be. For instance, consider the social anxiety example mentioned above. Normally, it could be difficult enough entering a room filled with people. You might agonize over what you want to say or pay attention to your appearance to guarantee that you make a good impression. These difficulties can be compounded by a natural tendency to turn neutral cues into threats and focus on threats to the exclusion of positive experiences. When introducing yourself to a new person, you may be more inclined to interpret his reaction as one of dissatisfaction. His face may bear a stronger resemblance to a scowl than to a neutral expression; his voice may seem more critical; and his behaviors that you interpret as negative may loom larger in your mind than do his affable gestures of cordiality.

The way you attend to your environment governs your experience. Therefore, it makes sense that you should try to ensure your interpretations are accurate prior to entering an anxiety-provoking situation. Scientific literature has identified some core areas of attention that are affected in people with high levels of anxiety. Let's review them.

Disengagement from Threat

Several studies have suggested that individuals with anxiety have trouble directing their attention away from threat. Therefore, if your environment contained multiple types of things—some positive, some neutral, some threatening—then you would be more likely to look at the threatening aspects for longer periods of time, which would prevent you from attending to other parts of your environment (that is, the neutral or positive parts).

In one study (Cisler and Olatunji 2010), participants with and without fears of contamination underwent a series of attentional tasks. In one such task, participants viewed two boxes displayed on a screen. Inside each box was a picture with one of the following valences: threat, disgust, or neutrality. So, participants could see a threatening picture on the left side of the screen and a neutral picture on the right side of the screen, a neutral picture on the left side of the screen and a disgusting picture on the right side of the screen, and so forth. Each set of pictures was briefly shown on the screen; then the pictures disappeared and a symbol appeared in one of the boxes. The participant then clicked on a button corresponding to the symbol. The results of the study demonstrated that those with higher levels of contamination fear exhibited more difficulty in disengaging from threat, because when the symbol appeared on the other side of the screen from a threatening picture, it took them longer to direct their attention to the symbol. In other words, their attention was fixed on the place where the threatening picture had been.

Eventual Threat Avoidance

Another very interesting phenomenon concerns what eventually occurs when someone looks at a threat for a longer period of time. We know that anxious individuals have an initial tendency to direct their attention toward threat, but then what happens? Recent research suggests that people tend to avoid threatening stimuli after the initial attraction. One study (Koster et al. 2005) found that when threatening images were presented for 500 milliseconds, anxious participants were quick to attend to them, but during longer time periods (1,250 milliseconds or more), the same participants exhibited greater avoidance tendencies.

Collectively, the evidence suggests that cognitive biases are anxiety's best friend. Let's look at an example. Imagine that you arrive at a party where you don't know most of the other partygoers. One of the first things you might notice is a partygoer frowning, the host's apparent lack of interest, or the glare of the person standing next to you. Next, you feel unable to maintain prolonged contact with these daunting experiences, compelling you to shift your attention elsewhere (perhaps prompting you to look down at your shoes or check your phone for new messages). It appears as if this cognitive bias can be divided into two stages. The first stage poises you to learn that the situation is predominantly dangerous by focusing exclusively on negative information (frowns, lack of interest, glares). The second stage guarantees that these negative experiences are the only pieces of information you will glean from the environment, as your eventual avoidance of the perceived threat prevents you from observing anything that may contradict your initial negative impression (for example, many of the partygoers look like they are enjoying themselves, and some have smiled at you).

How Changing Your Habits Prepares You to Deal with Frightening Situations

With these cognitive biases in mind, we can now take a look at a fascinating new study that has direct implications for improving anxiety. We showed in chapter 6 that mindfulness meditation is one potential way of correcting cognitive biases; however, other techniques have been developed from an *implicit* emotion regulation framework. Remember, implicit emotion regulation refers to those ways by which we manage our emotions unconsciously. One such technique is attention bias modification, which refers to a host of attention exercises designed to train your attention away from negative threats and toward positive stimuli.

A typical attention bias modification treatment session involves observing faces presented on a screen. Some of these faces have judgmental expressions, some have neutral expressions, and others have positive expressions. Then the faces are replaced by symbols, and you must locate a certain symbol. Using the logic of the cognitive bias studies mentioned above, this treatment assumes that if you have an anxiety disorder, you will direct your attention to the face with the most negative expression first. Therefore, the target symbol is programmed to more often appear in the location of a face with a positive expression. Over time, you become better at paying attention to faces with positive expressions. In this way, repeated practice with attention bias modification tasks often reduces attention biases toward threat.

Heeren et al. (2012) recruited participants with social anxiety disorder to enter one of three attention training conditions before giving a two-minute impromptu speech about a negative emotional experience, which would be video recorded. These three training conditions taught the participants to use their attention in very different ways. In the attend to positive (AP) condition, participants were trained to direct their attention to warm, welcoming faces 80 percent of the time, whereas in the attend to negative (AN) condition, they were trained to notice disapproving faces 80 percent of the time. The last condition was a control in which people were trained to attend to both faces 50 percent of the time and to receive no particular bias one way or the other. The researchers measured both subjective anxiety, as experienced in the speech task, and behavioral displays of anxiety. It was found that the AP condition led to reductions in both subjective distress and behavioral displays of anxiety compared to the AN condition. Moreover, the AP condition resulted in far fewer behavioral displays of anxiety relative to the control condition.

Overall, these results are consistent with the picture we presented earlier. Attention biases toward threatening stimuli aren't productive by any means. A mind that's too vigilant for danger is unable to assess its environment accurately. By using mindfulness and attention training programs to address these biases, you will be in a better position to process the positive experiences that are part and parcel of your everyday environment.

Using Attention Games to Quell Your Anxiety

The therapeutic effect of cognitive bias modification has roots in the science of emotions. Moreover, this type of help is easily implementable in the context of other treatments. It can complement techniques that span mindfulness meditation to exposure exercises, which you will learn more about in the next chapter.

One of the great things about cognitive bias modification is that it can be conveniently used with an app! Here are some we have found:

- Mood Mint: https://itunes.apple.com/gb/app/mood-mint-boost-your-mood/id634210028?mt=8

- PsychMeUp! http://www.mindhabits.com/mobileapps.php

- Personal Zen: https://itunes.apple.com/us/app/personal-zen/id689013447?mt=8

Two of these apps, PsychMeUp! and Personal Zen, are available for free. Take a look at them to see whether any fits your needs. For the purposes of this book, we encourage you to download a cognitive bias modification app. With this technology, you will be able to practice cognitive bias modification techniques anywhere!

Outsmarting Anxiety Skill #7:
Develop adaptive habits for long-term
regulation of your emotions.

Suggested Practices

Now we will explain how to use cognitive bias modification apps as a stand-alone strategy as well as to complement other strategies. Make use of this on a daily basis, and don't be too hard on yourself if you forget. As we say in the mindfulness tradition, just redirect your focus to where it should be!

Exercise 8.1: **Stand-alone Cognitive Bias Modification** As a first step, download the app of your choice. Try to practice the cognitive bias modification modules three times a day in a quiet location or when you are on the go. This is an excellent technique to practice when you are on a subway, when you are waiting in line, or simply whenever you feel a lull in the day. Remember, repetition is key! This is a form of training, after all. Just as infrequent exercise doesn't produce noticeable results, you won't achieve the full benefit from occasional use of this app. Take some time to get familiar with the app and figure out what times of the day are most conducive to its use.

Exercise 8.2: **Cognitive Bias Modification and Exposure Practice** Although you will learn more about advanced exposure practice in the next chapter, you can already integrate what we described earlier in this chapter in the context of exposures. We know that cognitive biases prevent you from taking in certain information that's key to accurately assessing your environment. Predispositions to see your world through dark-colored classes will shape how you feel and react to situations you initially perceived as anxiety-provoking.

First, identify a major fear that you have been struggling with. It could be a social situation, a scary object (such as a spider), or even alarming body sensations (such as panicky feelings). Once you come up with a scenario you want to work on, try the following:

1. Plan on a time when you can encounter your situation. For example, it could be deciding to attend a party to which you were invited or climbing up a tall ladder if heights make you nervous.

2. Right before you confront this situation, practice the cognitive bias modification module of the app. We recommend

that you go through it at least once, but more practice with it would be even better. This will prime you to be less reactive to threatening information and learn more about the positive or nonthreatening experiences within your environment.

3. Last but not least is the exposure itself. Place yourself in the feared environment while mindfully attending to what's occurring around you. Remember to pay attention to the here and now; don't attempt to avoid unwanted emotions or experiences. We recommend that you embrace them in an accepting and nonreactive manner. By doing this, you will be in a much better position to learn and realize that the situation might not be as dangerous as you initially perceived.

Exercise 8.3: **Cognitive Bias Modification and Mindfulness Practice**   One of the difficulties many people have when they first practice mindfulness is maintaining sustained concentration. It's of course very easy to get lost in your thoughts and be pulled out of the present moment by things that appear threatening. We will now show you how cognitive bias modification apps will give you a heads-up when it comes to mindfulness exercises.

1. Similar to practice 8.2, it will be important that you use the cognitive bias modification module at least once, preferably more times, before you practice your mindfulness exercises. By so doing, you will be able to be less distracted by threatening stimuli or negative thoughts and more likely to nonreactively and nonjudgmentally remain in the present moment, which is the overall purpose of mindfulness.

2. After your practice with the cognitive bias modification app, try practicing the mindfulness exercises in chapter

6. Sometimes people doing the mantra breathing exercise find that they can be distracted by other thoughts or things in their environment, and for anxious people, this usually happens when they believe they notice something negative. This time you will be in an even better position to foster mindfulness. Remember that you can use techniques such as the inhale-exhale practice, in which you slowly vocalize your mantra as you breathe in and breathe out. Practice your meditation exercise for ten minutes once per day after using the cognitive bias modification module. You will cultivate stronger focus and be better able to master your anxiety by being in the present moment.

***

In this chapter, we reviewed some additional scientific literature on cognitive biases toward threat showing that anxious individuals have trouble disengaging from dangerous stimuli initially but tend to avoid it later on. This is the exact attention process that exacerbates anxiety, but luckily, cognitive bias modification training can help. Not only do these training interventions target cognitive biases, they can be integrated with other exercises, letting you benefit even more. Continue to use these exercises as we move onto the next chapter, which is about exposure. Combined use of all the techniques we have mentioned thus far will lead to greater gains and help you master your anxiety.

chapter 9

Emotional Avoidance

There's a reason people tend to avoid what they dislike: it's unpleasant. Why would anyone in their right mind actively seek out what they fear? Common sense prevents people from taking unnecessary risks, such as willingly rushing into the middle of a highway filled with speeding cars or walking into a pit of venomous snakes; we know that doing so will likely result in a complete disaster.

Although plenty of situations are clearly dangerous, the threat your emotions communicate to you is often exaggerated. Indeed, although experiencing anxiety can be unpleasant, trying to escape from anxiety rarely results in anything good. This chapter will integrate what you have learned about emotion regulation and elaborate on the basic principles of exposure.

How Emotional Avoidance Does More Harm Than Good

Let's take a step back to remember how anxiety is maintained over time. In addition to physiological symptoms, anxiety is associated with overly cautious thoughts about the presence of danger and avoidance behaviors. Imagine you are walking across the street and you hear what sounds like a speeding car. A natural reaction would be for you to anticipate danger and experience fear. This strong emotion tells you to get out of harm's way. If there really were a car, then your anxiety would be adaptive in encouraging you to avoid the car. This avoidance of something potentially dangerous leads to a form of learning called *negative reinforcement* (see chapter 3). According to the principles of negative reinforcement, the sense of safety you experience after avoiding something that may have been dangerous makes you more convinced that it was in fact dangerous. This works well for real threats and is incredibly adaptive; however, this process can go awry pretty quickly if you are not careful.

Imagine what would happen if you were crossing the street and heard what sounded like a speeding car, but this time it was just the sound of a loud television. What would you feel? Relief! Glad to know that you were no longer in the presence of impending doom, you would likely turn off your internal alarm clock, and your anxiety would diminish over time. It wouldn't be all that beneficial for your anxiety to continue, as there was no real threat to which you needed to respond. But this is exactly what happens in people with high anxiety: their fear persists despite there being little evidence of threat. In other words, even though the speeding car isn't really there, your mind acts as if it were.

You will still learn about the situation irrespective of whether a threat exists. If you encounter an anxiety-provoking situation and run the other way, you are teaching yourself that the situation is dangerous. Your brain will notice that you are escaping some situation in which you feel anxious and will continue to believe some underlying threat is present. This means that, in the future, your brain will repeat this response tendency by turning on your internal alarm clock and using fear to persuade you to avoid the situation. It doesn't matter whether the danger is illusory or real: avoidance teaches your brain to act as if it were real.

So, why not eliminate avoidance? That seems simple enough in theory, but in practice it can be tricky, because avoidance offers short-term relief. It feels good to remove yourself from the prospect of delivering a speech in front of a large crowd or to avoid a nasty-looking spider by crossing the street. Avoidance can be seductive, but it's rarely a permanent solution. The long-term effects of avoidance are negative, because it prevents you from learning information about your environment that would discredit your negative beliefs. To change your response to anxiety-provoking situations, you will have to change your reliance on avoidance.

Being Safe vs. Being in the Present Moment

Avoidance isn't always as conspicuous as you might think. There are obvious examples of avoidance, such as fleeing a room filled with people or refusing to enter a crowded subway car, but there are also more subtle types of avoidance. For example, you might refrain from maintaining eye contact while talking to someone new at a party. Such ways of gaining relief or avoiding facing the situation head-on are known as "safety behaviors" or "avoidance strategies." They may lessen your initial anxiety, but they are just as bad as the full-fledged avoidance behaviors described in the previous section. Like those behaviors, they prevent you from learning more about your surrounding environment and teach you to fear the situation.

This is the great difficulty with anxiety. People often expose themselves to various fearful situations, yet their anxiety persists over time. That's why there's a critical distinction between being "safe" and being in the present moment in the presence of fear. When trying to be safe, you avoid fully accepting the situation and thus dealing with your fear; as a result, your fear stays strong.

This principle has been well documented in the scientific literature. For example, one study investigated the effect of exposure therapy on individuals with claustrophobia (Powers, Smits, and Telch 2004). Part of this treatment involves having people enter a small chamber. In one condition of the study, participants had the option of using avoidance strategies (such as opening a window or unlocking the door). In another condition, participants were *required* to use these avoidance strategies. In a third condition, these avoidance strategies were unavailable (that is, participants had to fully accept the fact that they were locked in a small chamber, with no means of gaining relief from their anxiety). Results of this study demonstrated, perhaps surprisingly, that ultimately the third group of participants had much less anxiety about being in the small chamber than either the first or second group. In fact, there was almost no difference in anxiety between the participants in the first and second groups. In light of this, the authors of the study argued that it's not necessarily the *use* of avoidance strategies but their availability that keeps people anxious about certain situations. In other words, you are more likely to continue to be anxious about a situation if you think that you might eventually *need* to use an avoidance strategy.

This suggests that if you want to reduce your anxiety, you shouldn't seriously entertain safety behaviors as an option. Therefore, it will be critical to foster emotional acceptance, which you can do by way of mindfulness. In the exercises that follow, we will distinguish two types of *fear objects*: external and internal. External fear objects are those feared situations and feared stimuli that are directly observable. For people with social anxiety, for example, public speaking is an external fear object. Internal fear objects can be slightly trickier to identify, as they can include physical symptoms (such as shortness of breath) or even thoughts (such as worry). People with generalized anxiety disorder tend to experience excessive, uncontrollable worry about multiple areas of their life and future uncertainty. As we mentioned before, worry has been conceptualized as a harmful emotion regulation strategy used to avoid unwanted emotions, which can train you to perceive future uncertainty as intolerable.

Because it's difficult to physically expose people to the things they worry about, researchers have developed innovative techniques to apply the principles of exposure therapy to repetitive negative thinking. In one study of people with symptoms of generalized anxiety disorder (Lee and Orsillo 2014), some participants were asked to mindfully focus their attention on their breath. Other participants were instructed to listen to relaxing music or let their thoughts wander to whatever topic they pleased. After undergoing these different treatments, participants were given an emotional Stroop task to measure their cognitive flexibility, or the ability to switch between thinking about two different concepts or to simultaneously think about multiple concepts, which as you learned in chapter 2, is important for overcoming avoidance. To refresh your memory, in this task, participants are asked to state the color of words with different emotional valences (negative, positive, and neutral). Often it takes anxious people longer to state the color of the word if it's threatening or dangerous, because they are automatically drawn to the content of the word. Sometimes they even say the word instead of stating the color.

The results of this study showed that those undergoing the mindfulness session were more likely to perform well on this task, thereby exhibiting greater cognitive flexibility. As we mentioned in chapter 5, avoidance is often associated with rigid emotion regulation strategies such as repetitive negative thinking. Having more flexibility in your responses to emotions is frequently linked to better mental health outcomes. Instead of reacting negatively to an unwanted emotion or a concern about an upcoming event, you can adopt strategies that foster greater acceptance and less avoidance of worry triggers. In the next section, we will show you how to use the principles of exposure and mindfulness to your advantage. Hopefully, you will be in a position where you can avoid less and accept more!

Outsmarting Anxiety Skill #8:
Let go of safety behaviors and avoidance strategies.

As you have learned, letting go of safety behaviors and not shying away from anxiety-provoking situations will foster a more accepting attitude and, thereby, alleviate your anxiety. However, there are different strategies that you can use depending on whether you want to take on a fear that's outside of you or a fear that's within you. In chapter 3, we presented the basics of emotional avoidance and how exposure can help combat anxiety. In the following exercises, we will incorporate techniques from the scientific literature on emotion regulation to enhance exposure exercises. Furthermore, the following practices are divided into two groups: one to help you deal with external fears and one for internal fears. Different strategies will be presented to show you how to accept the uncomfortable emotions associated with external or internal fears.

Suggested Practices: External Fears

We have all heard phrases such as "face your fear" and "confront your anxiety." Indeed, facing your fear or confronting your anxiety can be pretty difficult, for a number of reasons. In the first place, finding the motivation to approach a scary scenario head-on can require a great deal of effort. In the second place, there are many cases when you actually experience the feared situation all the time but never seem to get comfortable with it. Take social anxiety, for example. Unless you lock yourself in your room all day, it's nearly impossible to avoid social encounters. They occur at the grocery store, in class, at work, and almost anytime you walk down a street. Social situations are indeed ubiquitous. So why do people with social anxiety still experience dread if they are constantly exposing themselves to them? As we have highlighted throughout this chapter, the answer is avoidance. From leaving the social encounter altogether to refraining from maintaining eye contact, there are hundreds of ways to avoid fully experiencing the situation. The following practices will help you foster emotional acceptance by way of exposure without avoidance.

Before you begin these practices, review the guidelines we provided in chapter 2. It's important that you be consistent and patient. Practice daily, and be forgiving with yourself if you make a mistake!

Exercise 9.1: **Identify Your Avoidance and Safety Behaviors** Before beginning exposure, it's important to learn in what ways you use avoidance. Any ordinary behavior—crossing your arms or holding onto your drink with a firmer grasp—can be transformed into a safety behavior. It all depends on the *function* of the behavior. How do you know whether a certain behavior counts as a form of avoidance? You can test yourself by noticing what you tend to do in a feared situation. Here is your guideline: an avoidance behavior is anything you do to reduce your anxiety or control the situation. Use the format below (worksheet available at http://www.newharbinger.com/34169) to help you determine what behaviors you tend to rely on.

Situation →	Anxious Emotion →	Avoidance Behavior
1.		
2.		
3.		
4.		
5.		
6.		
7.		
8.		
9.		
10.		

Be very observant when you do this, and write down your responses soon after testing yourself. Safety behaviors can be subtle and thus difficult to detect, which is why it's important to spend some time figuring out which ones are specific to you.

Exercise 9.2: **Make a Fear Hierarchy**   Another important precursor to exposure is the development of a fear hierarchy, which you can create using the format below (worksheet available at http://www.newharbinger.com/34169).

List ten situations you tend to avoid. On a scale of 1 to 100, rate each one according to the level of distress, anxiety, or emotional discomfort you feel in that situation.

0–9:   No anxiety; calm; relaxed

10–39:   Mild anxiety; alert; able to cope

40–59:   Moderate anxiety; some trouble concentrating

60–89:   Severe anxiety; thoughts of leaving

90–100:   Very severe anxiety; extreme fear

Then, on a scale of 1 to 100, rate each situation according to how frequently you avoid it.

0–9:   Never avoid

10–39:   Avoid once in a while

40–59:   Avoid sometimes

60–89:   Usually avoid

90–100:   Always avoid

Then put those situations in order, with the highest numbers at the top and the lowest numbers at the bottom.

It will be key that you approach your fears in a systematic way. If you were learning how to swim for the first time, we wouldn't throw you into the deep end without flotation devices and hope for the best. Instead, you would practice at the shallow end until you built up confidence to tread into deeper and deeper water. Eventually, you would be able to swim laps across the whole pool from the deep to the shallow end without a problem. You need to approach your anxiety in a similar fashion: start with some of the less fearful situations and then work your way up to the most fearful ones.

Exercise 9.3: **Exposure Without Avoidance**   Now we enter the exposure itself. The principle is simple enough. All you really need to do is encounter your feared situation, but this time you will do it in a way that you have rarely done before. Let's illustrate with a few examples.

Example 1

Imagine that you have a fear of heights (also known as acrophobia). Most people who have this fear avoid looking out of windows while in tall buildings, rarely use ladders, and refuse to travel by plane. A fear hierarchy for acrophobia might have at the bottom something like looking out of a second-story window. At the top would be something far more frightening, such as riding a roller coaster. Whatever the steps in your hierarchy, it will be important to move from the bottom to the top in a systematic way so that you complete these exercises *repeatedly* and *without avoidance*.

For instance, a first step would be to look down at the ground from your second-story window three times a day for a week. Furthermore, you should do so without looking away, strengthening your grip on the windowsill, or distracting yourself in any way. Fully embrace the experience. If you do this enough, you will feel much more comfortable in this situation. A next step would be to practice this technique in a more daunting environment. Try this procedure again on the different floors of a tall building. Start with the fifth floor and then work your way up to the tenth. Do this repeatedly and without avoidance. Try to do it not just once or twice a week, but several times each day. Also, be cognizant of whether you are doing subtle things to avoid or control your anxiety. In the end, you may be in a much better position to ride the roller coaster without feeling so much dread.

Note that the goal of this practice isn't for you to feel no anxiety whatsoever. It's okay if you are a little nervous before riding the roller coaster. The objective is for you to become much more comfortable in these situations so that your life isn't limited by anxiety.

Example 2

Let's now imagine that your main complaint is social anxiety. We can use the same principles here. Again, we are going to focus on exposure to social situations *repeatedly* and *without avoidance*. A fear hierarchy for social anxiety might have at the bottom something like talking to a neighbor whom you don't know very well. At the top would be something far more frightening, such as giving a speech before a large audience.

A first step would be to have a brief conversation with your neighbor, except this time, no avoidance! Look the person in the eye, be comfortable with long pauses (they are okay!), and don't try to rehearse what you want to say. You need to convince your brain that social situations aren't dangerous by acting as if there's no reason to use safety behaviors. From there, gradually work on public speaking. Start by giving talks to yourself in the mirror. It's okay if you feel somewhat silly. In fact, that can work to your advantage, as it will get you used to feeling self-conscious. Again, do this three times a day for at least a week. The more you practice it, the more comfortable you will feel.

Once you begin to make progress, you can even incorporate intentional faux pas into your social encounters. Try paying for a cup of coffee using only change, or try walking backward down a busy street and singing out loud. By acting comfortably in situations that would normally seem awkward or daunting, you will restructure your mind to downplay the consequences of social blunders. What's the worst that can happen if you pay for a coffee in nickels and pennies? If people on the street stare at you, then so what? What you initially perceive will happen is often very different from what actually happens. Give yourself the opportunity to react differently to your anxiety, and you will learn how little some of these social situations matter in the long run. And practice, practice, practice! Repeatedly expose yourself without avoidance and you will train yourself to enjoy social situations rather than fear them.

Suggested Practices: Internal Fears

Just because you can't see it in front of you doesn't mean that it's not there. Your thoughts, emotions, and physical symptoms all can be potent sources of anxiety. You have learned how repetitive negative thinking strategies such as worry and rumination increase your distress over time, given their function as forms of avoidance. Now it's time to apply mindfulness to the situations you would usually worry about.

Exercise 9.4: **Mindful Observation**   Remember that techniques such as suppression and avoidance have a paradoxical effect. If you worry about an upcoming event and respond by trying to rigidly control or suppress your thoughts, your efforts will backfire! You may be able to avoid your worries in the short term, but they will surely return. And so this cycle repeats over and over again.

By reacting to your worries and judging them to be catastrophic, you prolong your distress and anxiety. In chapter 2, we encouraged you to maintain a mindful disposition by directing your attention to your breath. This time, try to extend mindfulness to worrying. Whenever a negative thought appears in your mind, don't try to analyze it or react to it. Instead, treat it as what it really is: a thought.

Whenever you experience worry, use your mantra (see chapter 6) to redirect your attention to the present moment. Because worry is a future-oriented thought process, this can be difficult to do, but remember that with practice and patience you can gain mastery over worry. Using your mantra will help you be mindful when observing negative thoughts.

Exercise 9.5: **Eliminate Your Safety Behaviors** If you experience generalized worry, you likely often procrastinate. Procrastination is a type of avoidance in which less urgent matters are prioritized over more urgent tasks. Common examples of procrastination are constructing to-do lists, completing minor tasks that are ancillary to the main project, and delaying work on difficult tasks. To counteract this indirect emotion regulation strategy, you should undertake the more difficult aspects of your tasks earlier on. Although they might be initially aversive, you will find that if you approach them in a nonreactive manner you will be more likely to focus on the concrete goals that must be accomplished in the present moment. Don't make lists; just do it!

People who experience high levels of worry also often seek reassurance. Reassurance-seeking entails attempts to minimize the discomfort surrounding future uncertainty by soliciting advice. Over time, this maladaptive strategy prevents you from learning that future uncertainty need not be overwhelming and insurmountable. By taking more initiative and making decisions without frequently turning to others, you will train yourself to perceive uncertainty as far more tolerable.

The function of a behavior dictates its utility for your emotions. Social support can be an excellent tool to help you cope with stressful events, and devoting large amounts of time to personally meaningful projects can often be very profitable. However, there are instances when these behaviors are more harmful than helpful. If you are performing them to avoid unpleasant emotions, then it might be helpful to take a step back and reflect. Perhaps these actions are reinforcing your perceptions that future uncertainty is threatening. Therefore, you should accept worrisome thoughts in a nonreactive manner rather than feeling compelled to seek reassurance or to put off doing something you don't want to do. By eliminating these safety behaviors, you will be in a better position to regulate your emotions more flexibly and learn more adaptive information about your situation.

✺ ✺ ✺

In this chapter, you learned more about the role of avoidance and its deleterious effects. There's certainly more to exposure than just exposure itself! Exposure to anxiety-provoking experiences needs to be done in a certain way: repeatedly and without avoidance. This is true whether your anxiety is driven by your thoughts or by the things and situations you encounter. Just as physical exercise increases bodily strength, frequent practice of these exposure exercises will give you greater mastery over your anxiety and facilitate more flexible emotion regulation. Remember to be patient with yourself, and use the exercises in this chapter to extend what you have accomplished so far with the skills provided in the earlier chapters.

chapter 10

Making a Habit of Mindfulness and Emotion Regulation

W e know, both from our own experiences and from the experiences of people we have worked with, that it's easy to dwell in guilt, regret, sadness, or bitterness (past-focused emotions) or stress, anxiety, worry, or tension (future-focused emotions). Unfortunately, spending too much of our lives outside the present moment adversely affects our well-being and ability to flourish. Throughout this book, we have presented scientifically based ways that emotion regulation and mindfulness can positively influence your life. Although none of the strategies and tips will cure your anxiety, all of them, when used consistently and reliably, will help you achieve a productive balance by flexibly managing your emotional experiences and meaningfully reducing your anxiety. To what degree these ideas and tips will promote change in your life depends entirely on your commitment to the work. We haven't intended to suggest in any chapter that emotion regulation and mindfulness efforts should entirely overtake your life (that would be counter-productive and antithetical to the very idea of mindfulness itself), but we hope that you will find ways to integrate into your everyday life at least one or two of the skills presented in this book, at a pace that works well for you.

Outsmarting Anxiety Skill #9:
Learn the integrated model of
emotion regulation and mindfulness
to successfully overcome your anxiety.

In writing this book, we set out to present a unified approach to managing your anxiety, one that uses both emotion regulation and mindfulness. Each of these approaches has a great deal of scientific and practical merit in its own right. In combining them to promote greater emotional well-being, it's important to remember that emotion regulation strategies help you know *what* you can do to manage your emotions—alter the type, duration, frequency, or context of your emotions—and mindfulness informs *how* you go about doing that: with purposeful intention, focused attention, and a nonjudgmental attitude (Shapiro et al. 2006; Cisler et al. 2010). The idea underlying an integrated framework of emotion regulation and mindfulness for addressing anxiety is that mindfulness training not only promotes increased attention and emotion regulation but also enhances your overall sense of self and well-being (Bränström and Duncan 2014).

The skills presented in each chapter are meant to synthesize and distill the scientific literature on emotion regulation and mindfulness into an accessible format for you to incorporate into your everyday life. Some may have seemed basic or easy, whereas others may seem overly difficult or out of reach. After reading this last chapter, we encourage you to reflect on the nine skills and highlight the ones that are less intuitive and require a deeper understanding or more practice.

1. Paying attention to your anxiety

2. Confronting, rather than avoiding, your anxiety

3. Avoiding common thinking traps

4. Flexibly responding to your emotions

5. Reducing conscious and unconscious threats to your emotional well-being

6. Accepting your emotions

7. Developing adaptive habits for long-term regulation of your emotions

8. Letting go of safety behaviors and avoidance strategies

9. Learning the integrated model of emotion regulation and mindfulness to successfully overcome your anxiety

People have a tendency to skim or read a book once and then set it down, but we encourage you to use this book and the skills we've reviewed as a guide to mastering your anxiety over the long term (as opposed to only right now or some discrete time period in the future).

Seeing the Big Picture with Your New Skills

As you work at incorporating tenets of this book into your life, there are a few important points to remember. First, *it's impossible to fail* at using any of the skills or, more broadly, at addressing your anxiety. If you adopt a truly nonjudgmental stance toward your present-moment experiences, then your efforts, regardless of their outcome, are all that matter. In essence, each time you mindfully practice a skill (or set of skills), such as working toward confronting your anxiety or accepting your emotions, you contribute to your overall ability to live life more fully and flourish. Another way to think about this is like investing in a savings account. No matter how small the amount of money you deposit into your account, it still contributes to the overall growing balance and your financial stability. If you happen to go a week, a month, or even a year without making a deposit, you can rely on the previous investments you have made to your account with the understanding that you still have plenty of opportunities to further contribute. As long as you integrate mindfulness and emotion regulation skills into your life, they will become more fluid and automatic ways of flexibly responding to your emotions, your internal experiences, and your external world.

Second, *most everything in life is about how you perceive it.* We have talked about this throughout the book, but the main idea is to develop, through emotion regulation and mindfulness practices, new frameworks for interpreting your everyday life. A simple, yet intuitive, example of this is how you view rain. When you learn that there's rain in the forecast, do you tend to loathe it, or do you welcome it for its benefit? On one hand, rainy days are usually cold and gloomy. The rain can slow down your commute and leave you struggling to simply stay dry while dashing between work and errands. On the other hand, rain is as much a benefit as it is a discomfort, if not more so! It nourishes plants and vegetation, it renews water sources, and it's the primary basis for life and growth. Rain even increases overall work productivity, because there are fewer distractions on rainy days (Lee, Gino, and Staats 2014; Richards 2014). This isn't to suggest that you should enjoy each and every rainy day but to teach you to recognize *how you perceive your life experiences* and *how your interpretations impact your moment-to-moment emotions.* There's often value in pain and discomfort, which doesn't imply that you should seek those experiences, but when they do arise, you can look for the opportunity to reframe them and gain perspective.

Third, and most importantly, *everyone is capable of change.* To believe otherwise perpetuates a harmful line of thinking, encourages you to accept your perceived weaknesses, and lowers your self-esteem. Change is a learning process (remember learning about learning in chapter 3?), and this book is meant to help you learn the skills necessary to capably respond to your emotions and manage your anxiety—both moment to moment and long term. Unlike diets or guides to investment, emotion regulation and mindfulness don't offer specific or stepwise formulas for achieving your goals. Instead, they offer you tools to adaptively focus your attention, disrupt your unhelpful thinking habits, decrease your reactivity to internal experiences, increase your tolerance of negative emotions, and enhance your ability to accept and reappraise your emotions. The key to making true changes in managing your emotions and anxiety is practicing these skills not only when the moment calls for it but also when change is not urgent or not absolutely necessary.

Using This Book in Your Daily Life

If you are reading this book for the first time, we encourage you to find time to read it again, and again, and yet again! It's not that this book is the only authority on mindfulness, but it contains a set of skills that you have (hopefully) committed to learning and utilizing in your everyday life. We recommend you read this book multiple times so that you can expertly integrate mindfulness into your life and to more fully develop adaptive responses for regulating your emotions. The end goal is for this book to become a coaster for your coffee, but only when you have been able to apply what you read to mastering your anxiety.

The themes presented throughout this book require both a deep understanding of the concepts and numerous opportunities for practicing them. We don't, and you most certainly shouldn't, expect yourself to perfectly understand, let alone accurately apply, every tip on the first try. The best way to use this book is to find benign opportunities to practice the skills, such as being mindful while brushing your teeth, while standing in a line, or during your morning commute. You can then purposefully look for opportunities to practice mindfully regulating your emotions, such as noticing when you feel jealous of a friend or loved one, when you have the urge to lash out at someone, or when you find yourself yelling angrily at the television when your favorite football team is losing. Once you have developed some mastery of these skills, apply them as well as you can to the moments when you most feel anxious. The skills may not help the first or even the tenth time you use them, but they eventually will. The more the skills become incorporated and ingrained into your ways of feeling, thinking, and behaving, the greater the benefit to your well-being.

Resources for Anxiety

New Harbinger Publications (https://www.newharbinger .com) has a great many books and self-directed workbooks on topics such as mindfulness, emotions, and anxiety. The websites of the Anxiety and Depression Association of America (http://www.adaa.org) and the Association for Behavioral and Cognitive Therapies (http://www.abct.org) can help you learn about specific anxiety disorders or find therapists in your area who are experienced in treating anxiety disorders. (Both of these organizations are based in the United States, but their websites have information on international resources.) Additionally, many larger universities offer reduced-cost or free therapy to community members. If you live near a university that has a mental health clinic (often part of the psychology department), we encourage you to call them to learn about their services. There are, of course, other ways of locating therapists in your area, such as a referral from your primary care provider, and we encourage you to use other resources as well.

A well-known form of psychotherapy for treating anxiety disorders is cognitive behavioral therapy (CBT). CBT is a scientifically tested type of psychotherapy that has proved effective for a number of anxiety and depressive disorders. Individuals who participate in CBT usually spend time focusing on present-moment concerns by using an active problem-solving approach. They learn to identify problematic ways of thinking; the relationship among thoughts, emotions, behaviors, and bodily sensations; and how to set goals to meaningfully reduce their anxiety symptoms. CBT is brief and time-limited, meaning it typically takes from eight to twenty-four sessions to complete, but the exact number of sessions will vary from individual to individual. The expectation for CBT is that you will use the skills you learn for as long as necessary to manage your anxiety, if not for life. Many of the ideas and skills presented in this book fit well with CBT and can be a useful starting point for discussion with a clinician.

"Mindfulness" encompasses several structured training programs, such as mindfulness-based stress reduction and mindfulness-based cognitive therapy, which have both shown promising results in terms of helping individuals decrease stress and increase well-being. Like emotion regulation, mindfulness is usually incorporated into various other therapies, such as CBT, dialectical behavior therapy, and acceptance and commitment therapy (ACT; Hayes, Strosahl, and Wilson 2011). It's beyond the scope of this book to review each of these forms of therapy, but know that mindfulness has been incorporated into many scientifically tested therapies that have shown strong potential for increasing your ability to manage and reduce your symptoms of anxiety. We encourage you to research these therapies to learn more about these various programs.

If you are interested in learning more about mindfulness in general or participating in nontherapeutic courses, we encourage you to research opportunities in your area. An Internet search for "mindfulness courses" is all but guaranteed to find you a wealth of options. There are also a number of academically oriented mindfulness centers at various universities around the country. These centers typically offer reduced-fee or low-cost mindfulness courses, either live (in-person) or online, for members of their community. There are also several for-profit businesses that offer mindfulness courses; although many are reputable, we encourage you to use good judgment.

Final Thoughts

Congratulations on having read this book! It took us years of study to bring you the information and ideas it contains. If there was some part of this book or a single piece of information that you enjoyed or found helpful, please track one or both of us down online to let us know. Similarly, if you found a particular topic (or even a single paragraph or sentence) difficult to understand, or if you think we got something wrong, please also let us know! We are invested in improving the way we teach people about their anxiety and how to best manage it using emotion regulation and mindfulness.

Whatever your motive for reading this book, we are glad that you have chosen to incorporate emotion regulation and mindfulness into your life. This book is one of many on this subject, but we think it offers a good start in terms of learning about your anxiety and how to better approach the management of your emotions in an integrated and comprehensive way. We believe that emotion regulation and mindfulness can be used by anybody, at any time, and for any reason. We sincerely hope that you will not only find value in what you have read but also pass on what you have learned to others.

Acknowledgments

We would like to express our gratitude and appreciation to the editors and staff of New Harbinger Publications. Their support and guidance were invaluable to the development of this book. We especially thank our team of editors—Melissa Valentine, Nicola Skidmore, and Angela Autry Gordon—for their special role in helping this book come to fruition. We also would like to specially thank Will DeRooy, our copy editor, for his conscientious and intelligent editing of our manuscript. Finally, we thank Stefan Hofmann, PhD, our friend and mentor, for writing the foreword to this book.

David H. Klemanski

I would like to extend my sincere thanks to my coauthor, Joshua Curtiss. Josh is an incredibly brilliant and gifted scholar, and he has a very bright future in psychology and academia! I could not have been more thrilled when he agreed to join me in writing this book, and I am grateful for the opportunity to work with him on a topic that's important to both of us.

I would also like to thank my parents, Henrietta and Guy Klemanski, and my sister, Dori Klemanski, all of whom have been my strongest advocates in life and my biggest supporters in my career (my mom even went so far as to cook and deliver to me dinners when she became concerned about the long hours I had been putting into writing this book!). Thank you as well to my many colleagues at Yale who have had a profound influence on my career. Special thanks to the late Susan Nolen-Hoeksema, PhD; Doug Mennin, PhD; Alan Kazdin, PhD; Dwain Fehon, PsyD; Seth Axelrod, PhD; and the many brilliant and special students with whom I have had the pleasure to work and teach.

Joshua E. Curtiss

Throughout this rewarding and arduous undertaking, I have appreciated the invaluable assistance of several important people. I would like to extend many thanks to my coauthor, David Klemanski, whose clinical acumen and brilliant insights have made this book what it is. I must also acknowledge Stefan Hofmann, PhD, an inspirational colleague and researcher whose contributions to the science of emotion regulation and mindfulness proved a valuable source for our book. Moreover, this accomplishment could not have been possible without the support of my wonderful parents. Finally, I am forever grateful to my loving wife, Stephanie Noble, for her incomparable brilliance, encouragement, and artistic ingenuity.

References

Aldao, A., and S. Nolen-Hoeksema. 2010. "Specificity of Cognitive Emotion Regulation Strategies: A Transdiagnostic Examination." *Behaviour Research and Therapy* 48 (10): 974–83.

Amrhein, C., P. Pauli, W. Dengler, and G. Wiedemann. 2005. "Covariation Bias and Its Physiological Correlates in Panic Disorder Patients." *Journal of Anxiety Disorders* 19 (2): 177–91.

Arch, J. J., and M. G. Craske. 2006. "Mechanisms of Mindfulness: Emotion Regulation Following a Short Breathing Induction." *Behaviour Research and Therapy* 44: 1849–58.

———. 2010. "Laboratory Stressors in Clinically Anxious and Nonanxious Individuals: The Moderating Role of Mindfulness." *Behaviour Research and Therapy* 48 (6): 495–505.

Arnsten, A. F. 2009. "Stress Signalling Pathways That Impair Prefrontal Cortex Structure and Function." *Nature Reviews Neuroscience* 10 (6): 410–22.

Baer, R. A., G. T. Smith, J. Hopkins, J. Krietemeyer, and L. Toney. 2006. "Using Self-report Assessment Methods to Explore Facets of Mindfulness." *Assessment* 13 (1): 27–45.

Bar-Haim, Y., D. Lamy, L. Pergamin, M. J. Bakermans-Kranenburg, and M. H. van Ijzendoorn. 2007. "Threat-Related Attentional Bias in Anxious and Nonanxious Individuals: A Meta-analytic Study." *Psychological Bulletin* 133 (1): 1–24.

Barnes, S., K. W. Brown, E. Krusemark, W. K. Campbell, and R. D. Rogge. 2007. "The Role of Mindfulness in Romantic Relationship Satisfaction and Responses to Relationship Stress." *Journal of Marital and Family Therapy* 33 (4): 482–500.

Beard, C. 2011. "Cognitive Bias Modification for Anxiety: Current Evidence and Future Directions." *Expert Review of Neurotherapeutics* 11 (2): 299–311.

Becker, E. S., M. Rinck, J. Margraf, and W. T. Roth. 2001. "The Emotional Stroop Effect in Anxiety Disorders: General Emotionality or Disorder Specificity?" *Journal of Anxiety Disorders* 15 (3): 147–59.

Bishop, S. R., M. Lau, S. Shapiro, L. Carlson, N. D. Anderson, J. Carmody, Z. V. Segal, S. Abbey, M. Speca, D. Velting, and G. Devins. 2004. "Mindfulness: A Proposed Operational Definition." *Clinical Psychology: Science and Practice* 11 (3): 230–41.

Borkovec, T. D., O. Alcaine, and E. Behar. 2004. "Avoidance Theory of Worry and Generalized Anxiety Disorder." In *Generalized Anxiety Disorder: Advances in Research and Practice*, edited by R. G. Heimberg, C. L. Turk, and D. S. Mennin. New York: Guilford Press.

Borkovec, T. D., W. J. Ray, and J. Stöber. 1998. "Worry: A Cognitive Phenomenon Intimately Linked to Affective, Physiological, and Interpersonal Behavioral Processes." *Cognitive Therapy and Research* 22 (6): 561–76. DOI: 10.1023/A:1018790003416

Bränström, R., and L. G. Duncan. 2014. "Mindfulness and Balanced Positive Emotion." In *Positive Emotion: Integrating the Light Sides and Dark Sides*, edited by J. Gruber and J. Tedlie Moskowitz. New York: Oxford University Press.

Brown, K. W., and R. M. Ryan. 2003. "The Benefits of Being Present: Mindfulness and Its Role in Psychological Well-Being." *Journal of Personality and Social Psychology* 84 (4): 822.

Byrne, A., and M. W. Eysenck. 1995. "Trait Anxiety, Anxious Mood, and Threat Detection." *Cognition and Emotion* 9 (6): 549–62.

Campbell-Sills, L., D. H. Barlow, T. A. Brown, and S. G. Hofmann. 2006. "Effects of Suppression and Acceptance on Emotional Responses of Individuals with Anxiety and Mood Disorders." *Behaviour Research and Therapy* 44 (9): 1251–63.

Chambers, R., B. C. Y. Lo, and N. B. Allen. 2008. "The Impact of Intensive Mindfulness Training on Attentional Control, Cognitive Style, and Affect." *Cognitive Therapy and Research* 32 (3): 303–22.

Cisler, J. M., and B. O. Olatunji. 2010. "Components of Attentional Biases in Contamination Fear: Evidence for Difficulty in Disengagement." *Behaviour Research and Therapy* 48 (1): 74–78.

Cisler, J. M., B. O. Olatunji, M. T. Feldner, and J. P. Forsyth. 2010. "Emotion Regulation and the Anxiety Disorders: An Integrative Review." *Journal of Psychopathology and Behavioral Assessment* 32 (1): 68–82.

Coffey, K. A., and M. Hartman. 2008. "Mechanisms of Action in the Inverse Relationship Between Mindfulness and Psychological Distress." *Complementary Health Practice Review* 13 (2): 79–91.

Corcoran, K. M., N. Farb, A. Anderson, and Z. V. Segal. 2010. "Mindfulness and Emotion Regulation." In *Emotion Regulation and Psychopathology: A Transdiagnostic Approach to Etiology and Treatment*, edited by A. M. Kring and D. M. Sloan. New York: Guilford Press.

Cucchi, M., V. Bottelli, D. Cavadini, L. Ricci, V. Conca, P. Ronchi, and E. Smeraldi. 2012. "An Explorative Study on Metacognition in Obsessive-Compulsive Disorder and Panic Disorder." *Comprehensive Psychiatry* 53 (5): 546–53.

Curtiss, J., and D. H. Klemanski. 2014a. "Factor Analysis of the Five Facet Mindfulness Questionnaire in a Heterogenous Clinical Sample." *Journal of Psychopathology and Behavioral Assessment* 36 (4): 683–694.

Curtiss, J., and D. H. Klemanski. 2014b. "Teasing Apart Low Mindfulness: Differentiating Deficits in Mindfulness and in Psychological Flexibility in Predicting Symptoms of Generalized Anxiety Disorder and Depression." *Journal of Affective Disorders* 166: 41–47.

Davidson, R. J. 2010. "Empirical Explorations of Mindfulness: Conceptual and Methodological Conundrums." *Emotion* 10 (1): 8–11.

Desrosiers, A., V. Vine, J. Curtiss, and D. H. Klemanski. 2014. "Observing Nonreactively: A Conditional Process Model Linking Mindfulness Facets, Cognitive Emotion Regulation Strategies, and Depression and Anxiety Symptoms." *Journal of Affective Disorders* 165: 31–37.

Dresler, T., K. Mériau, H. R. Heekeren, and E. van der Meer. 2009. "Emotional Stroop Task: Effect of Word Arousal and Subject Anxiety on Emotional Interference." *Psychological Research* 73 (3): 364–71.

Drost, J., W. van der Does, A. M. van Hemert, B. W. Penninx, and P. Spinhoven. 2014. "Repetitive Negative Thinking as a Transdiagnostic Factor in Depression and Anxiety: A Conceptual Replication." *Behaviour Research and Therapy* 63: 177–83.

Ehlers, A., and D. M. Clark. 2000. "A Cognitive Model of Posttraumatic Stress Disorder." *Behaviour Research and Therapy* 38 (4): 319–45.

Erisman, S. M., and L. Roemer. 2010. "A Preliminary Investigation of the Effects of Experimentally Induced Mindfulness on Emotional Responding to Film Clips." *Emotion* 10 (1): 72.

Forgas, J. P. 2014. "Can Sadness Be Good for You?: On the Cognitive, Motivational, and Interpersonal Benefits of Negative Affect." In *The Positive Side of Negative Emotions*, edited by W. G. Parrott. New York: Guilford Press.

Friedman, B. H., and J. F. Thayer. 1998. "Autonomic Balance Revisited: Panic Anxiety and Heart Rate Variability." *Journal of Psychosomatic Research* 44 (1): 133–51.

Frijda, N. H. 1986. *The Emotions.* Cambridge: Cambridge University Press.

Gilboa-Schechtman, E., E. B. Foa, and N. Amir. 1999. "Attentional Biases for Facial Expressions in Social Phobia: The Face-in-the-Crowd Paradigm." *Cognition and Emotion* 13 (3): 305–18.

Gross, J. J. 1998. "The Emerging Field of Emotion Regulation: An Integrative Review." *Review of General Psychology* 2 (3): 271.

———. 2008. "Emotion Regulation." In *Handbook of Emotions*, 3rd ed., edited by M. Lewis, J. M. Haviland-Jones, and L. Feldman Barrett. New York: Guilford Press.

Gross, J. J., and R. A. Thompson. 2007. "Emotion Regulation: Conceptual Foundations." In *Handbook of Emotion Regulation*, edited by J. J. Gross. New York: Guilford Press.

Gyurak, A., J. J. Gross, and A. Etkin. 2011. "Explicit and Implicit Emotion Regulation: A Dual-Process Framework." *Cognition and Emotion* 25 (3): 400–412.

Hansen, C. H., and R. D. Hansen. 1988. "Finding the Face in the Crowd: An Anger Superiority Effect." *Journal of Personality and Social Psychology* 54 (6): 917–24.

Hauser, M., F. Cushman, L. Young, R. Kang-Xing Jin, and J. Mikhail. 2007. "A Dissociation Between Moral Judgments and Justifications." *Mind and Language* 22 (1): 1–21.

Haybron, D. M. 2014. "The Value of Positive Emotion: Philosophical Doubts and Reassurances." In *Positive Emotion: Integrating the Light Sides and Dark Sides*, edited by J. Gruber and J. Tedlie Moskowitz. New York: Oxford University Press.

Hayes, S. C. 2004. "Acceptance and Commitment Therapy, Relational Frame Theory, and the Third Wave of Behavioral and Cognitive Therapies." *Behavior Therapy* 35 (4): 639–665.

Hayes, S. C., J. B. Luoma, F. W. Bond, A. Masuda, and J. Lillis. 2006. "Acceptance and Commitment Therapy: Model, Processes and Outcomes." *Behaviour Research and Therapy* 44 (1): 1–25.

Hayes, S. C., K. D. Strosahl, & K.G. Wilson. 2011. *Acceptance and Commitment Therapy: The Process and Practice of Mindful Change*. New York: Guilford Press.

Heeren, A., H. E. Reese, R. J. McNally, and P. Philippot. 2012. "Attention Training Toward and away from Threat in Social Phobia: Effects on Subjective, Behavioral, and Physiological Measures of Anxiety." *Behaviour Research and Therapy* 50 (1): 30–39.

Herbert, J. D., and E. M. Forman, eds. 2011. *Acceptance and Mindfulness in Cognitive Behavior Therapy: Understanding and Applying the New Therapies*. Hoboken, NJ: John Wiley & Sons.

Hill, C. L., and J. A. Updegraff. 2012. "Mindfulness and Its Relationship to Emotional Regulation." *Emotion* 12 (1): 81–90.

Hofmann, S. G., S. Heering, A. T. Sawyer, and A. Asnaani. 2009. "How to Handle Anxiety: The Effects of Reappraisal, Acceptance, and Suppression Strategies on Anxious Arousal." *Behaviour Research and Therapy* 47 (5): 389–94.

Hofmann, S. G., A. T. Sawyer, A. A. Witt, and D. Oh. 2010. "The Effect of Mindfulness-Based Therapy on Anxiety and Depression: A Meta-analytic Review." *Journal of Consulting and Clinical Psychology* 78 (2): 169.

Kabat-Zinn, J. 1994. *Wherever You Go, There You Are: Mindfulness Meditation in Everyday Life*. New York: Hyperion.

———. 2009. *Full Catastrophe Living: Using the Wisdom of Your Body and Mind to Face Stress, Pain, and Illness*. 15th anniversary ed., with a new introduction by the author. New York: Delta.

Kessler, R. C., W. T. Chiu, O. Demler, and E. E. Walters. 2005. "Prevalence, Severity, and Comorbidity of 12-month DSM-IV Disorders in the National Comorbidity Survey Replication." *Archives of General Psychiatry* 62 (6): 617–27.

Koster, E., G. Crombez, S. van Damme, B. Verschuere, and J. de Houwer. 2005. "Signals for Threat Modulate Attentional Capture and Holding: Fear-Conditioning and Extinction During the Exogenous Cueing Task. *Cognition and Emotion* 19 (5): 771–80.

Larsen, R. 2000. "Toward a Science of Mood Regulation." *Psychological Inquiry* 11: 129–41.

Lau, H. P. B., M. P. White, and S. Schnall. 2013. "Quantifying the Value of Emotions Using a Willingness to Pay Approach." *Journal of Happiness Studies* 14: 1543–61.

LeDoux, J. 2015. *Anxious: Using the Brain to Understand and Treat Fear and Anxiety.* New York: Viking.

LeDoux, J. E., and J. M. Gorman. 2001. "A Call to Action: Overcoming Anxiety Through Active Coping." *American Journal of Psychiatry* 158 (12): 1953–55.

Lee, J. J., F. Gino, and B. R. Staats. 2014. "Rainmakers: Why Bad Weather Means Good Productivity." *Journal of Applied Psychology* 99 (3): 504.

Lee, J. K., and S. M. Orsillo. 2014. "Investigating Cognitive Flexibility as a Potential Mechanism of Mindfulness in Generalized Anxiety Disorder." *Journal of Behavior Therapy and Experimental Psychiatry* 45 (1): 208–16.

Llera, S. J., and M. G. Newman. 2014. "Rethinking the Role of Worry in Generalized Anxiety Disorder: Evidence Supporting a Model of Emotional Contrast Avoidance." *Behavior Therapy* 45 (3): 283–99.

Lundh, L. G., and M. Sperling. 2002. "Social Anxiety and the Post-event Processing of Socially Distressing Events." *Cognitive Behaviour Therapy* 31 (3): 129–34.

National Safety Council. 2015. "Knowledge Is Power: Understanding Our 'Odds of Dying' Can Help Us Make Safer Choices, Says National Safety Council." http://www.nsc.org/learn/about/Pages/Understanding-Our-Odds-of-Dying-Make-Safer-Choices.aspx.

Newman, M. G., S. J, Llera, T. M. Erickson, A. Przeworski, and L. G. Castonguay. 2013. "Worry and Generalized Anxiety Disorder: A Review and Theoretical Synthesis of Evidence on Nature, Etiology, Mechanisms, and Treatment." *Annual Review of Clinical Psychology* 9: 275–97.

Nolen-Hoeksema, S., B. E. Wisco, and S. Lyubomirsky. 2008. "Rethinking Rumination." *Perspectives on Psychological Science* 3 (5): 400–424.

Öhman, A., and S. Mineka. 2001. "Fears, Phobias, and Preparedness: Toward an Evolved Module of Fear and Fear Learning." *Psychological Review* 108 (3): 483–522.

Ortner, C. N., S. J. Kilner, and P. D. Zelazo. 2007. "Mindfulness Meditation and Reduced Emotional Interference on a Cognitive Task." *Motivation and Emotion* 31 (4): 271–83.

Penney, E. S., and M. J. Abbott. 2015. "The Impact of Perceived Standards on State Anxiety, Appraisal Processes, and Negative Pre- and Post-event Rumination in Social Anxiety Disorder." *Cognitive Therapy and Research* 39 (2): 162–77.

Perkins, A. M., and P. J. Corr. 2014. "Anxiety as an Adaptive Emotion." In *The Positive Side of Negative Emotions*, edited by W. G. Parrott. New York: Guilford Press.

Pineles, S. L., and S. Mineka. 2005. "Attentional Biases to Internal and External Sources of Potential Threat in Social Anxiety." *Journal of Abnormal Psychology* 114 (2): 314–18.

Plumb, J. C., S. M. Orsillo, and J. A. Luterek. 2004. "A Preliminary Test of the Role of Experiential Avoidance in Post-event Functioning." *Journal of Behavior Therapy and Experimental Psychiatry* 35 (3): 245–57.

Powers, M. B., J. A. Smits, and M. J. Telch. 2004. "Disentangling the Effects of Safety-Behavior Utilization and Safety-Behavior Availability During Exposure-Based Treatment: A Placebo-Controlled Trial." *Journal of Consulting and Clinical Psychology* 72 (3): 448.

Richards, T. A. 2014. "The Paradox of the Rain: An Anxiety Parable." http://anxietynetwork.com/content/paradox-rain-anxiety-parable.

Rinck, M., E. S. Becker, J. Kellermann, and W. T. Roth. 2003. "Selective Attention in Anxiety: Distraction and Enhancement in Visual Search." *Depression and Anxiety* 18 (1): 18–28.

Roemer, L., and T. D. Borkovec. 1994. "Effects of Suppressing Thoughts About Emotional Material." *Journal of Abnormal Psychology* 103 (3): 467–74.

Safran, J. D., and Z. V. Segal. 1990. *Interpersonal Process in Cognitive Therapy*. New York: Basic Books.

Scherer, K. R. 2005. "What Are Emotions? And How Can They Be Measured?" *Social Science Information* 44 (4): 695–729.

Segal, Z. V., J. M. G. Williams, and J. D. Teasdale. 2002. *Mindfulness-Based Cognitive Therapy for Depression: A New Approach to Preventing Relapse*. New York: Guilford Press.

Shapiro, S. L., L. E. Carlson, J. A. Astin, and B. Freedman. 2006. "Mechanisms of Mindfulness." *Journal of Clinical Psychology* 62 (3): 373–86.

Teper, R., Z. V. Segal, and M. Inzlicht. 2013. "Inside the Mindful Mind: How Mindfulness Enhances Emotion Regulation Through Improvements in Executive Control." *Current Directions in Psychological Science* 22 (6): 449–54.

Treanor, M. 2011. "The Potential Impact of Mindfulness on Exposure and Extinction Learning in Anxiety Disorders." *Clinical Psychology Review* 31 (4): 617–25.

Tull, M. T., K. L. Gratz, K. Salters, and L. Roemer. 2004. "The Role of Experiential Avoidance in Posttraumatic Stress Symptoms and Symptoms of Depression, Anxiety, and Somatization." *Journal of Nervous and Mental Disease* 192 (11): 754–61.

Tversky, A., and D. Kahneman. 1974. "Judgment Under Uncertainty: Heuristics and Biases." *Science* 185: 1124–31.

Van der Does, A. W., M. M. Antony, A. Ehlers, and A. J. Barsky. 2000. "Heartbeat Perception in Panic Disorder: A Reanalysis." *Behaviour Research and Therapy* 38 (1): 47–62.

Wachs, K., and J. V. Cordova. 2007. "Mindful Relating: Exploring Mindfulness and Emotion Repertoires in Intimate Relationships." *Journal of Marital and Family Therapy* 33 (4): 464–81.

Wald, J., and S. Taylor. 2005. "Interoceptive Exposure Therapy Combined with Trauma-Related Exposure Therapy for Post-traumatic Stress Disorder: A Case Report." *Cognitive Behaviour Therapy* 34 (1): 34–40.

Wells, A. 2011. *Metacognitive Therapy for Anxiety and Depression*. New York: Guilford Press.

Wenzlaff, R. M., and D. M. Wegner. 2000. "Thought Suppression." *Annual Review of Psychology* 51 (1): 59–91.

White, K. S., T. A. Brown, T. J. Somers, and D. H. Barlow. 2006. "Avoidance Behavior in Panic Disorder: The Moderating Influence of Perceived Control. *Behaviour Research and Therapy* 44 (1): 147–57.

Yerkes, R. M., and J. D. Dodson. 1908. "The Relation of Strength of Stimulus to Rapidity of Habit Formation." *Journal of Comparative Neurology and Psychology* 18: 459–82.

David H. Klemanski, PsyD, MPH, is a psychologist and professor at Yale University where he directs the Yale Center for Anxiety and Mood Disorders, and the Yale Anxiety and Emotion Lab. He specializes in the classification and treatment of anxiety and mood disorders, and his research is focused on mindfulness and emotion regulation in anxiety and depression.

Joshua E. Curtiss, MA, is a doctoral researcher at Boston University and conducts psychology research at Yale University as a statistician. His interests include the use of innovative statistical modeling to address issues pertaining to the nosology of emotional disorders. Specifically, his research delineates emotion regulation deficits underlying anxiety disorders.

Foreword writer **Stefan G. Hofmann, PhD**, is a professor in Boston University's department of psychological and brain sciences clinical program, where he directs the Social Anxiety Program at the Center for Anxiety and Related Disorders.

FROM OUR PUBLISHER—

As the publisher at New Harbinger and a clinical psychologist since 1978, I know that emotional problems are best helped with evidence-based therapies. These are the treatments derived from scientific research (randomized controlled trials) that show what works. Whether these treatments are delivered by trained clinicians or found in a self-help book, they are designed to provide you with proven strategies to overcome your problem.

Therapies that aren't evidence-based—whether offered by clinicians or in books—are much less likely to help. In fact, therapies that aren't guided by science may not help you at all. That's why this New Harbinger book is based on scientific evidence that the treatment can relieve emotional pain.

This is important: if this book isn't enough, and you need the help of a skilled therapist, use the following resources to find a clinician trained in the evidence-based protocols appropriate for your problem. And if you need more support—a community that understands what you're going through and can show you ways to cope—resources for that are provided below, as well.

Real help is available for the problems you have been struggling with. The skills you can learn from evidence-based therapies will change your life.

Matthew McKay, PhD
Publisher, New Harbinger Publications

If you need a therapist, the following organization can help you find a therapist trained in cognitive behavioral therapy (CBT).

The Association for Behavioral & Cognitive Therapies (ABCT) Find-a-Therapist service offers a list of therapists schooled in CBT techniques. Therapists listed are licensed professionals who have met the membership requirements of ABCT and who have chosen to appear in the directory.

Please visit www.abct.org and click on *Find a Therapist*.

For additional support for patients, family, and friends, please contact the following:

Anxiety and Depression Association of American (ADAA)
please visit www.adaa.org